German Cooking
made easy
Savory German dishes prepared in the traditional way

Galahad Books · New York City

German Cooking made easy published by Galahad Books, New York City

This edition published by arrangement with 'Round the World Books Inc., New York, New York

Series designed by Margaret Verner

Additional pictures pages 14, 17 and 19 courtesy of the German Wine Information Service, Toronto, Canada.

Recipes page 90 and additional information contributed by the German Wine Information Service, Toronto, Canada and CMA, New York.

Library of Congress Catalog Card Number: 79-52185

ISBN: 0-88365-416-4

Printed in the United States of America

Contents

Germany at the table

INTRODUCTION

A word that the Germans themselves use to describe many aspects of German life, is "gründlich", meaning solid. Like most national characteristics, the German reputation for extreme thoroughness and seriousness has been exaggerated. But no one – and particularly not the Germans themselves – would deny the German passion for organizing everything down to the smallest detail, or their profound distrust of improvisation. This applies not only to their cars and cameras, but to their cooking as well.

German cooking may not possess the fantasy and imagination of Italian cooking, or the delicate refinements of French cooking, but this does not mean that German cooking is bad. On the contrary, German home cooking (which the Germans call "gut bürgerliche Küche", or good plain cooking) is honest, down-to-earth, simple and substantial; it is perfectly in tune with the earnest spirit of German life. Traditionally, the Germans eat five times a day. But this custom is slowly disappearing as the traditional belly of the honest burgher has given way to the slimmer lines that doctors and the younger generation approve.

The day begins, or at any rate used to, with a breakfast consisting of crisp, fresh "Semmeln", the famous milk rolls. These are served with butter, honey and a three-minute egg accompanied by a large pot of coffee. In the south of Germany it is accompanied by an equally large pot of tea.

The second breakfast is served at around eleven o'clock. In nobler times, the rich shipowners in Hamburg and Bremen, the aristocrats in their castles, and the stately lords of Berlin, Munich and Frankfurt, made a grand ritual of this meal. It was customary to go to a famous restaurant that served such delicacies as smoked goose breast,

Specialities from North Germany against a background of the impressive old Trendelburg Castle.

smoked salmon, or a plate of oysters with a bottle of white Rhine wine or a bottle of sparkling Sekt, the German version of Champagne. (It is said that Sekt never tastes so marvelous as at eleven o'clock in the morning.)

The common man, for his part ate hot sausages and potato salad, along with a glass of beer, for his second breakfast; the farmer out in the country ate thick slices of dark bread and cured ham with a few small glasses of brandy called "schnaps". The brandy assumed several different forms from region to region: in the north of Germany, it was a crystal-clear gin which tasted of Kornbrand (grain brandy); in the south of Germany it was either inviting, aromatic Kirschwasser (distilled from stewed cherries) or Zwetschenwasser (distilled from stewed plums). In the country, the second breakfast is still a strictly followed tradition, but in the cities it has been gradually reduced to a simple sausage sandwich which children take to school and adults take to work.

By noon the stomach has just barely had time to begin to growl, but it is time for "Mittagessen", which is actually dinner and a substantial meal. It begins with soup, preferably made with noodles or dumplings, and is followed either by a roast, accompanied by potatoes and vegetables or a salad, by a hearty casserole dish, or by sauerkraut with different kinds of sausages.

At five o'clock, as the afternoon draws to a close, it is time for "Kaffee mit Kuchen", coffee with cakes and tarts. This "Kaffee" is the German counterpart of the English "tea time". The coffee hour is treated like a complete meal. In old-fashioned German families, the table is set with beautiful lace or embroidered tablecloths and with the best silverware and china. The German housewife puts her heart and soul into these homemade cakes and tarts. Even those who

don't happen to be very good cooks are almost invariably good bakers.

In the shopping centers of the large cities and the small towns of the provinces alike, the coffee hour is the most pleasant part of the day. The "Konditoreien", those renowned pastry shops, fill up with housewives who are out shopping, with couples, and even with men who come alone. Unlike their American counterparts, German men never seem to mind being seen in the genteel atmosphere of a pastry shop enjoying a cup of coffee and a slice of cake. In fact it is very difficult at the coffee hour to find a seat around one of the small bright tables.

In many German cities, there are famous pastry shops with a tradition that goes back more than 150 years. The shop windows are arranged with cakes, fruit pies, cream pies, and chocolate tarts that could tempt the resolve of a saint. After a day of this much culinary indulgence, it would be surprising if

there were much appetite left for the evening meal. An "Abendbrot", a simple, cold meal, is the usual choice. It consists of several kinds of bread accompanied by cold meats and sausages. Often there are also different kinds of cheeses, such as Emmenthaler (commonly known as Swiss cheese, but actually a native of Bavaria). Beer is always the faithful companion.

All the ingredients for the "Abendbrot" are usually bought in the "Feinkost-geschäfte", better known to us as a delicatessen. The German delicatessen is a unique contribution to good eating, with a bewildering choice of cold meats and sausages, beautifully displayed and deliciously aromatic. These are foods for which Germany is unsurpassed. Of course, the almost mythical American hot dog had its origins among these numerous spicy frankfurters. There are also many different kinds of beer sausages, with or without spices, onions and garlic, but always

marvellously tasty. Then there are the many varieties of the appetizing liver sausage: the hearty Berliner sausage and the light Saxon sausage. There are dark blood sausages, sometimes made with kidneys or tongue, and white "Weisswurst" made with aromatic green garden herbs. There is priceless ham from Westphalia which is smoked over a smoldering juniper berry fire that gives it a particular and distinctive aroma.

Besides all these, the delicatessen carries ready-to-serve salads made with meats, creamy potatoes or the delicate meat of a calf's head that has been marinated in sour cream and then minced until smooth and creamy. For those who would rather have fish there are delicacies like smoked salmon and smoked eel, or Bismarck herring in a sour, piquant sauce. There are also "Rollmops", which are sour herring wrapped around sour pickles. And if all this weren't enough of a choice for a light supper, there is still cold trout in aspic, or smoked trout, or fine lobster from Helgoland, the small rocky island off the northern coast of Germany.

Apart from their fame in the art of sausage-making, the Germans excel in a number of other gastronomic specialties. One of the first to come to mind is sauerkraut. The Ancient Romans probably knew the principles of how to make it. Finely shredded, salted cabbage was placed in pots or vats allowing a special fermentation to take place which gave the cabbage a slightly sour taste, but left it easily digestible all the same. This art seems to have disappeared from Europe with the fall of the Roman Empire. But it was brought back by the Asiatic hordes who invaded Eastern Europe in the Thirteenth and Fourteenth Centuries. The Asiatic invaders were very well acquainted with the art of making sauerkraut, and since cabbage is one of the hardiest vegetables grown, sauerkraut actually formed the basis for the alimentation of the whole of Eastern and Central Europe, from Rumania to Alsace on the eastern border of France. Today, the area surrounding

Stuttgart grows millions of cabbages, all of which will disappear into earthenware and wooden vats for a time, to reappear as aromatic white sauerkraut.

Sauerkraut is a very versatile dish in Germany; it is served in winter and summer, in the humblest kitchens and the best restaurants, with ham, bacon, partridge, goose and with different kinds of sausages. Hot sauerkraut with frankfurters is the traditional snack eaten in train stations and wayside restaurants along the turnpikes and highways.

One of the castle-hotels near the Neckar river.
The cook here serves his guests authentic dishes from the region.

Another specialty of German cuisine is the delightful assortment of fresh baked cakes and tarts, and sweet and spiced breads. Gingerbread, honeybread and spiced gingerbread are never absent from any Christmas table. Every year, a few weeks before Christmas, the Christmas market opens in the cities and small villages. The Christmas tree is put up in the middle of the market square of the picturesque old towns. Nearby, the grey tower of the cathedral disappears in the December mist, and behind the small windows of the Medieval city hall, glows the golden crown of candles. The market stalls grouped around the Christmas tree sell Christmas ornaments, flowers and, especially, cookies. Heart or star shaped, these special cookies taste of honey and spices, are decorated with pink and white sugar borders and have ribbons so that they can be hung on the Christmas tree. According to tradition, each child who goes to the

market with his mother or grandmother always returns home carrying one of these cookies around his neck.

German cooking is known for still another specialty, the goose. This has acquired the status of a sort of national fowl. These loud cackling birds can almost always be seen walking in long lines through the small German villages. The goose is said to be a difficult fowl to prepare, being too large for one person and too small for two (which gives a good impression of the German appetite.) The Germans prepare goose in a number of different ways, but they prefer it stuffed with apples and prunes. Smoked goose breast is an especially refined German delicacy that ranks with smoked salmon and smoked trout. The plentiful goose fat is never wasted. It can be melted and blended with grated apples to make a spread for dark, somewhat sour, farmer's bread, and it is used to fry the most delicious potatoes in the world.

One cooking art the Germans fully understand is that of roasting game. Though a crowded country, Germany still has a large reserve of forests and woods, including the famous Black forest, the forests of the Eifel, Hunsrück, the mountain chains of the Weser and the hills of Northern Bavaria. Game, such as deer and wild boar, rabbit and pheasant, still roams these forests freely, and in the wilder forests of Bavaria there are even capercaillie.

Game tastes best when prepared in the old traditional manner: roasted and accompanied by a piquant sauce of wine and spices, by stewed "Preisselbeeren" (bitter-sour small red berries found in the forest) or by spicy or savory wild brown mushrooms.

Germans love to eat out. One never has to look very far to find a "Gasthof", an intimate restaurant with a wine or beer cellar. The lovely old handcarved signboard outside points the way for the hungry and thirsty just as it has for centuries. The simple wooden stools covered with checkered cushions are arranged around an unpainted wooden table lit by candles or soft lamplight. The service is in the hands of a maiden in a flowered dress and apron who brings beer in large earthenware mugs, or carries trays laden with glasses of red wine and plates of sauerkraut, sauerbraten or delicious trout.

The old German tradition of the "Stammtisch", the friends' table, still exists in these friendly eating places. Every evening a group of men who know each other exclusively from patronizing other "Gasthofs" or beer and wine cellars get together to drink and enjoy each other's company.

Wine

Casteller Schlossberg

Vineyards in the Ahr region

While Germany sometimes seems awash on a sea of beer, we should not forget that it is also a land of wine, where rows of grapevines cling to the sunny southern slopes of the hills. There are golden white wines which smell of spring flowers or the blooming apple trees that edge the vineyards, and sometimes also of mignonette and hawthorn.

There are maiden-like light, fresh Mosel wines, temperamental golden wines of a surprising bouquet from the Rheingau, full-bodied and languid wines from Rheinhesse, luxurious, heady wines from Rheinpfalz and racy, spicy wines, bottled in flat, round bottles on the shores of the Main.

The sparkling wines drunk on the comfortable terraces along the Rhine, under the shade of pruned chestnut trees remain very much in the spirit of Germany's old castles. The delicate golden Rhine wines can still be drunk on the stately white ships that glide through the landscape of hills, forests and castles along the bank of that romantic river. These pale aromatic wines provide the perfect balance for the solid and serious German cooking.

German wines grow principally along the banks of the Rhine and along a few of its tributaries. The great majority are white wines, but there are a few red wines to be found here and there. From North to South, German wine areas produce the following types:

Ahr
(the towns of Alternahr and Neuenahr): red wines of fairly good quality.

Mosel
(with both tributaries, Saar and Ruwer): simple to very good white wines.

The best Mosel wine comes from the area between the villages of Neumagen and Traben-Trarbach.

Rhine
the best known wine areas are:

Mittelrhein (between Sankt Goar and Assmannshausen): white wines of fair to rather good quality; red wines from the area near Assmannshausen.

Rheingau (between Rüdesheim and Hochheim): white wines which are sometimes of exceptionally good quality. The best German wines come from this area, for example, Schloss Johannisberg and Schloss Vollrads. In England, Rhine wines are often called "Hock"; the name derives from the wine village, Hochheim, which provided the wines that Queen Victoria loved.

Rheinessen (between Mainz and Worms): fairly strong white wines of fair quality; red wines from Inghelheim.

Rheinpfalz (between Worms and Speyer): heady white wines mostly of fair quality, but some of very good quality, such as those from the area near Dürkheim.

Main
Most of the wines from this area, and especially from the area surrounding Würzburg, are called "Frankenweine", good white wines. They arrive in flat, round bottles.

A South German vineyard in the Autumn sun.

Württemberg

THE OFFICIAL QUALITY EXAMINATION

The most striking feature of the new German Wine Laws from July 1971 is the classification of German wines into three groups according to quality – Tafelwein, Qualitätswein and Qualitätswein mit Prädikat.

The Tafelwein group consists of those wines which, as grape must, did not attain the minimum level of maturity, measured as specific gravity, necessary to be included in the next highest group. Tafelwein is not subject to any official examination other than the normal food laws as enforced by the Public Analyst.

Qualitätswein, on the other hand, has to fulfil very exacting requirements. Not only does it have to result from officially recognized grape varieties grown in registered vineyards, it has also to undergo an official examination. The wine-grower is obliged to have his wines analyzed at an official laboratory and then tasted by an official commission. The purpose of this tasting is to establish the value or quality of a wine in terms of points. According to the number of points gained a wine can be classified as being a normal quality wine or a Kabinett, Spätlese, Auslese, Beerenauslese or Trockenbeerenauslese. These are the only designations permitted nowadays, with the exception of "Eiswein", a subsidiary descriptive term allowed only in conjunction with one of the compulsory terms. Two further bottles of the wine tasted by the commission are sealed and retained by the authorities in the event of future reclamations making a retasting necessary. The chemical analysis can be regarded as a wine's identity card, while the official certification number, the so-called A.P.Nr., printed on the wine label, is the consumer's guarantee that the wine has been officially tasted and approved.

The tasting commission can not only reject a wine completely, it can also relegate a wine into a lower category. Each of these decisions has to be made in writing so that the wine-grower has the chance of submitting a claim to the Appeals Commission where the wine is examined once more should he not agree with the decision reached by the tasting commission.

QUALITY GRADE: SPECIALLY GRADED QUALITY WINE

Five grades of highest quality specially graded wines are allowed and mentioned on the label. A wine will only be eligible if it is fully matured and possesses a harmonious balance between sweetness and fruitiness.

The "must weight" (or the grape's original sugar content) is even higher than the ordinary wines, and in no circumstances may sugar be added to the juice. Each one of the five specially graded wines is checked for its time in vintage, method of harvesting, and the ripeness of the grapes. A declaration of the grade combined with the control number must be shown on the label.

Kabinett – an elegant, fully ripened wine, harvested at the normal time. "Normal" in Germany as a rule means October, a time when the grapes have long been gathered in the rest of Europe. It is this lengthy, slow ripening time which increases German wine's unique characteristics.

Spätlese – these wines come from grapes harvested after the normal picking period. They are distinguished by a special elegance and ripeness and are appealingly "round and delicious".

Auslese – produced from the fully ripe grapes which are specially sorted from the rest and pressed separately. Auslese wines reveal their elegance through their ripeness and full bouquet and are unquestionably ideal for a special occasion.

Beerenauslese – a further increase in quality where the wine is made from ripe and over-ripe berries separated by hand. This results in a wonderful, mature, fruity and full wine which possesses an unmistakable flowery aroma and a color like amber.

Trockenbeerenauslese – this is wine of the very finest quality. Only grapes shrivelled like raisins are pressed, offering significant characteristics in appearance and taste.

Eiswein – this is a very special type of wine similar to the last two grades. It is made from grapes, the water content of which has been frozen by the first frost, and the inner concentration, rich in sugar and aroma, is squeezed out.

HOW LONG DO GERMAN WINES KEEP?

What are the criteria determining a German wine suitable for laying down for a long period? To begin with, it is advised against laying down wines low in acidity and extract, small vintages, wines from bulk producing varieties and from sites with light soils as well as wines tasting dull even in their youth. They will bring disappointment with increasing age.

In general, **red wines** (15% of the German production) are more suitable for long storage than are whites. If the red wines are not light table wines but full-bodied ones in higher quality classes, they must certainly be stored before they reach an optimum ripeness for drinking. A minimum storage period of five years is to be expected for Burgundies.

White wines which are powerful, full, rich in acidity, but not quite dry, are the most suitable for long storage. The higher the quality class, the better the keeping properties of the wines. High extract with a goodly level of acidity and sweetness is the guarantee that the wine will have a long life. The selected harvestings of Riesling, rich in extract, usually reach their optimum development in regard to taste between 5 and 25 years for Spätlesen, between 10 and 50 years for Auslesen and the higher qualities such as Beerenauslesen and Trocken-beerenauslesen between 20 and 100 years.

The **grape variety** also plays an important part in determining the suitability of a wine for laying down. The best of the white wines for long storage is the Riesling and the best of the reds the Spätburgunder (Pinot noir).

A further criterion for the keeping properties of a wine is the way in which the harvest was brought in and the wine developed prior to bottling.

Finally, it must be emphasized that the question ''How long do German wines keep'' can only be answered in conjunction with the way in which they are stored. Wine can only age ideally when stored in a dark cellar under stable conditions at an even temperature between 12 and 16°C, if possible. The volume of air in the bottle should be the minimum. Today wine from a good winery is developed and bottled in such a way that it does not lose its stability on being stored temporarily at a temperature of more than 20°C. However, on storing wines for several years the temperature should not rise above 16°C.

Rheinhessen

Franken vineyards

How to read the German wine label

Labels on German wines are said to be among the most attractive in the world... and also the most elaborate to read. Once you understand the basic label pattern (as shown in the following generic illustration) you should know exactly what's inside the bottle:

The **region** from which the wine comes.

The vintage or **year** when the wine was made.

The village from which the wine comes. Here, the hypothetical village is **Winzerdorf.** And it becomes the name of the wine by adding an "er" at the end (just like a man from New York is a New Yorker and from London, a Londoner).

The vineyard **Rebberg** surrounding Winzerdorf where grapes were grown from which the wine was made.

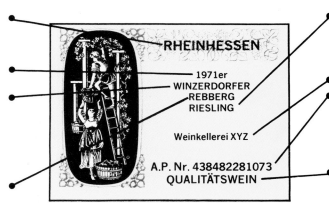

RHEINHESSEN

1971er
WINZERDORFER
REBBERG
RIESLING

Weinkellerei XYZ

A.P. Nr. 438482281073
QUALITÄTSWEIN

The variety of grape used to make the wine; here, a Riesling Germany's premier grape. Other white varieties include Silvaner, Müller-Thurgau, and Ruländer.

The name of the producer or shipper.

Official quality testing number, given by the government to wines passing rigid examination. Found only on **Qualitätswein** and **Qualitätswein mit Prädikat.**

Refers to category of wine in bottle. Here, a **Qualitätswein.**

Beer

Beer has been the national drink of Germany beyond memory. German beer, especially Hamburg and Bremen beer, has been famous for centuries. As far back as the Fifteenth and Sixteenth Centuries it was already being exported to England. Many cities still produce their own beer brewed in the same way as in the Middle Ages: through natural fermentation which gives it a rich, velvety texture and a distinctive taste. Berlin Weiss, which is flavored with a bit of raspberry juice, and Kolsch are good examples.

Strict purity regulations which govern the brewing of beer and its sale are of the greatest importance in as much as they insure that any beer coming onto the market must contain nothing but malt, hops, water and yeast; any artificial ingredients or chemical additives such as are used in other countries to increase for instance the frothiness of the beer or its keeping quality or give it a more brilliant appearance are expressly banned in the Federal Republic.

The use of unmalted grain as for instance rice or maize is also not allowed in Germany. This is why there have never been any "beer scandals" of any kind in the Federal Republic. Thanks to these stringent purity regulations the Germans drink beer which in respect of quality, full-bodied flavor and, above all, for its digestibility is scarcely equalled by any other beer.

Living up to its reputation for being "the Land of the Beer and the Breweries", the Federal Republic maintains at two universities facilities for the study of brewing. There are also many foreign students among the budding brewers. Once graduated and after some practical experience many a German brewer or engineer specializing in brewing technology goes abroad.

Many breweries and particularly in North and South America have German names – evidence of the great reputation enjoyed, not only by German beer, but also by the training in brewery science available in the Federal Republic. There exists in the Federal Republic quite a number of societies and institutes devoted to research into brewing problems.

Beer-drinking traditions

In the north of Germany, where the winters are cold and damp, it is customary to warm up with a small glass of "Schnaps" before starting on the beer. The brandy assumes several different forms from region to region: in the south of Germany it is either inviting, aromatic Kirschwasser distilled from stewed cherries or Zwetchenwasser distilled from stewed plums; in the north of Germany it is a crystal-clear gin with a strong juniper berry aroma tasting of "Kornbrand" (corn brandy).

German beer drinking reaches its pinnacle in the October "Beer Fest" in Munich. This Bacchanalian festival begins in the last week of September and lasts through the first week of October. It takes place in the Theresian meadows, which take their name from the Bavarian princess for whose wedding the feast was first held in 1810. The meadows are usually covered with enormous tents, in which people drink surprising quantities of beer from large earthenware steins which may hold up to two quarts. These are carried about by buxom "Mädchen" who manage to deal with four or five of these giants in one hand.

Roasted ox, chicken, sausages and grilled fish are devoured in vast quantities. The music of the street musicians dressed in short leather trousers gets louder and more insistent. Faces glow redder with beer and the carnival flavor.

Beer is brewed throughout Germany: even small provincial towns have their own breweries. A few of the exceptional beers:

Märzenbier: a light, golden brown and lively flavored beer which comes mostly from Munich.

Berliner Weiss: a light beer brewed from wheat through natural fermentation.

Altbier: a racy beer brewed through natural fermentation. It comes principally from Westfalen and Cologne.

Münchener: a fairly strong, dark beer from Munich.

Bockbier: dark, strong, and very aromatic beer which originally came from the small town of Einböck but is now brewed all over Germany.

Dortmunder: light, lively hop beer which comes from Dortmund.

A tall goblet Rhine wine and a delicious variety of German cheeses: an inseparable union.

HARD CHEESES

Distinguished by the high percentage (at least 60%) of dry matter they contain. Consequently, they can be stored for very long periods. Once cut, however, they must be protected from drying out. The hard cheese family includes "Allgau Emmental" (king of cheese), Chester (used almost exclusively for processing) and "Bergkäse", a mountain cheese.

Standard Types: Emmentaler, Chester

SCHNITTKÄSE (SLICEABLE CHEESE)

Has a dry-solid content, from 49% to 57%; ideal for slicing.

Standard Types: Tilsit, Gouda, Edam, Trappist

SEMI-SOFT (SLICEABLE) CHEESE

Has a dry content of from 44% to 55%. Although sliceable, it is softer than "Schnittkäse", and therefore often confused with other soft cheeses.

Standard varieties: Wilstermarschkäse, Steinbuscher, Edelpilzkäse, Butterkäse, Weisslacker.

SOFT CHEESES (WITH REDDISH TINGE)

Made by smearing outside of cheese with broth of moldproducing bacteria; marketed in many varieties, shapes; soft and supple; must consist of from 35% to 52% dry matter; if overripe, paste tends to run.

Standard types: Romadur, Limburg, Münster

MORE SOFT CHEESES

Apart from the so-called "Rotschmier" cheeses – the types which through the action of certain bacteria assume a reddish tinge and which have already been dealt with - (see under Romadur, Limburg and Münster), there is another group of soft cheeses with a moldy crust. To this category belong, not only the standard types of Camembert and Brie, but also a number of cheeses

which, though non-standard, are nevertheless widely known by such names as "wine cheese" and "breakfast cheese". Their fat content must not be less than 35% and no more than 52% of dry-matter.

SOFT CHEESES WITH A MOLDY CRUST

CAMEMBERT: one of the best-known of all cheeses, loved throughout the world for its mild, aromatic flavor. Popular too because of its availability in handy, individual portions.

Camembert has a thin layer of mold and reveals only a few holes when its surface is cut. Ranges from three-quarters fat to double cream.

BRIE: closest relative to Camembert; usually eaten in a less ripe stage; has very aromatic odor and a taste that ranges from slightly sour to mildly piquant.

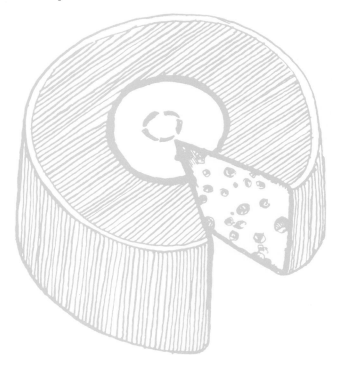

FRESH CHEESES

Designed for immediate consumption, without a ripening process; made from pasteurized milk with lactic acid cultures and rennet; particularly popular because of their dollar-related value. Fat standard ranges from double-cream to low-fat.

CURD CHEESE is made of skimmed milk, buttermilk, whole milk, or whole milk with the addition of cream. It is the cheapest source of high-grade protein in our food. Curd cheese should be soft, delicate and supple; it should have a slightly sour milk taste. Curd cheese is highly suitable for a number of different cheese dishes; it may be used for baking or served as sweet hors d'oeuvre or as a hearty main dish.

SCHICHTKÄSE (layer cheese) is a kind of curd cheese, distinguished by its several layers – always one of skimmed milk curd alternating with one of full-fat milk curd. Taste is similar to that of ordinary curd cheese; consistency is delicate, supple, but not runny. Most dairies make curd and layer cheeses.

SOUR CURD CHEESE

The product from sour milk curd, sold in many varieties, has a high protein content. Good value for money. Some varieties mold-covered; others, yellow.

CHEESE PRODUCTS

Made by adding other dairy products or foodstuffs, without melting the cheese base.

PROCESSED CHEESE

Made by melting cheese – various hard or sliceable types. Other dairy products then are added, such as cream, butter, or whey powder. Foodstuffs can also be added, such as ham, mushroom, paprika. (Such additions must be kept within legally determined limits).

The cheese processing industry is known for its wide variety of products, which keep almost indefinitely, are ready to eat at all times, and satisfy practically all tastes. So many processed items are available it's almost an impossibility to name all of them!

A SMALL DICTIONARY OF BREADS:

Fünfkornbrot – Five Grain Bread
produced from rye, wheat, yeast, barley, corn and millet.

Grahambrot – Graham Bread
Wholemeal bread in which the bran is separated from the flour, ground very finely and then added once more to the ground meal, baked without any baking aids (yeast).

Knäckebrot – Cracker Bread
a liquid dough is baked in thin layers very quickly at high temperatures, then dried, which makes the crisp bread a durable baked good. A large range available.

Kommissbrot
Tin or sandwich loaf of very finely ground rye flour with smooth crust.

Kümmelbrot – Caraway Seed Bread
Tin or sandwich loaf with soft crust of whole shredded wheat with germ baked in. Coarse grained.

Landbrot – Country Bread
mainly of rye flour, baked dark brown mainly in flat round loaves.

Leinsamenbrot – Linseed Bread
Whole shredded wheat meal loaf with whole seeds of the linseed plant baked in.

Pumpernickel
Whole meal rye bread, which receives its deep, dark brown coloring by extended baking.

Weizenkeimbrot – Wheat Germ bread
Whole wheat grains are shredded and baked together with freshly sprouted wheat germs. Particularly moist and fine grained.

Westfälisches Vollkornbrot – Westphalian Whole meal Bread
Dark brown rye bread with whole grains, tin shaped and sliced.

Zwieback
the name means it is baked twice. Made of wheat flour, milk and butter. Must be brittle and baked through.

Meats

GERMAN GOURMET MEATS

There is the greatest variety of sausages in Germany. Different regions and towns are famous the world over for their particularly good products and specialties, among them for example, Westphalia, Brunswick and Schleswig-Holstein.

No cold supper would be complete without at least four different kinds of sausage on the table to be eaten with bread and butter, and frequently the choice is even greater. This is not difficult to understand once you have tasted the varieties available.

Basically, sausages can be broken down into three categories:

Kochwurst

This consists of pieces of meat which were cooked before the sausage was made. The best known Kochwurst types are: Leberwurst, fine and coarse; Palatinate Leberwurst; herbe Leberwurst; calf Leberwurst, goose Leberwurst; Landleberwurst; Gutsleberwurst and many other kinds; Leberkäse; Blutwurst (a form of blood pudding); Thüringer Blutwurst; Zungenwurst (tongue sausage); Sülzwurst (aspic sausage).

Brühwurst (Scalded sausage)

These are made from very finely chopped or ground beef, pork or veal, strongly smoked and kept below boiling point during the making. The following are important types: Bierschinken, Bierwurst, Fleischwurst, Jagdwurst, Lyoner, Mortadella, Regensburger and Wiener Würstchen, Bockwurst, Original Frankfurter Würstchen, Saftwürstchen.

Rohwurst (Spreadable sausage)

Larder sausages of raw, finely minced, lean meat and fat, cooled by air and smoked. In this family are: Braunschweiger, coarse and fine; Mettwurst, coarse and fine; Streichmettwurst; coarse and fine Teewurst; Rügenwalder Teewurst.

Germany is also renowned for its variety of hams – both raw and boiled which are for the most part produced from the pork leg. Depending upon the time production takes place, a differentiation is made between Summer and Winter ham.

Some of the most prominent are: Westphalian ham, Holstein ham on the bone, Black Forest ham, Coburg ham and Nut ham.

Salted herring and apple salad—see recipe page 28

The most tempting and enticing sight in Germany is the spacious, festively lit window of the delicatessen, where the salads are artfully displayed.
There is a delightful choice of potato salads, meat salads with sausages, salads with fish and different sorts of vegetable salads. All these are served at the 'Abendbrot', the evening meal of cold cuts and salads which is customary in Germany.
Whether by accident or design, salads are the perfect companion for the substantial, nutritious, dark brown German bread, and for the foamy glass of beer that completes the inseparable trio. German salads are hardly the light little trifles that the French serve with their food. Nor are they the cold, crisp fresh snacks that we eat as a side dish. John Barrymore's famous remark that 'there are two things that a woman can make out of nothing: a hat and a salad' has nothing to do with the German variety. The Germans eat their salads as a real meal and expect them to be substantial enough to be worth the effort. And, in contrast to ourselves, the Germans love soft, velvety salads. Nowhere else in the world can you get such creamy potato salads and meat salads as in Germany. The secret of this velvety smoothness is thick sour cream.

Salted herring and apple salad

Hamburger Heringstöpfchen

4 servings

½ cup sour cream
1½ teaspoons vinegar
1½ teaspoons sugar
½ teaspoon horseradish
1 (5 oz.) jar pickled herring,
   drained and **sliced**
1 medium onion, **sliced**
1 apple, peeled, cored and
   sliced
   Lettuce leaves
   Pimiento strips
   dill pickles

Combine sour cream, vinegar, sugar and horseradish; blend well. Let stand 10 minutes. Combine herring, onion, apple and pickles; toss lightly. Add dressing; mix lightly. Chill. Serve on lettuce leaves. Garnish with strips of pimiento.

Shredded cabbage salad

Krautsalat

4 servings

2 cups water
1 teaspoon salt
4 cups shredded cabbage
   (1 small head cabbage)
1 teaspoon caraway seed
4 slices bacon, diced
1 medium onion, chopped
¼ cup vinegar

Bring water, with salt added, to a boil. Add cabbage and caraway seed. Simmer for 10 minutes; drain and cool. Cook bacon in skillet until lightly browned. Add onions and cook until golden. Add bacon pieces, onions, 4 tablespoons of bacon drippings, and vinegar to cabbage. Toss until well mixed. Serve immediately.

Sauerkraut salad

Sauerkrautsalat

4 servings

1 (16-oz.) can sauerkraut,
   drained
2 green apples, peeled and
   chopped
½ cup chopped sour pickles
1 medium onion, chopped
2 tablespoons chopped fresh
   dill
2 tablespoons chopped parsley
1 teaspoon salt
2 tablespoons sugar
2 tablespoons lemon juice
¼ cup salad oil

Put sauerkraut in salad bowl; separate with fork. Add apples, pickles, onion, dill, parsley, salt, sugar, and lemon juice. Mix well. Heat oil and pour over salad; it should sizzle. Toss until well mixed. Chill. Serve cold.

Beet and endive salad

Rote-Beten-Salat

4 servings

1 (8 oz.) can sliced beets
2 Belgian endives, sliced and
   cut up or 1 small head of
   chicory, broken into small
   pieces
1 apple, grated
1 small onion, chopped
2 tablespoons horshradish
2 egg yolks
1 tablespoon lemon juice
3 tablespoons sour cream
½ teaspoon prepared mustard
1 teaspoon sugar
1 teaspoon salt
¼ teaspoon black pepper
½ clove garlic, minced
3 tablespoons oil

In a large salad bowl, combine beets, endive (or chicory), apple, onion, and horseradish. In a small bowl, mix egg yolks, lemon juice, sour cream, mustard, sugar, salt, pepper, and garlic. Mix well. Using a wire whisk, slowly add oil, drop by drop, to dressing mixture. Blend thoroughly. Pour over salad; toss well. Chill.

Salted herring and beet salad

Roter Heringssalat

4 servings

4 (1 lb. jar) salted or schmalz herring fillets cut into ½″ cubes
½ cup diced cold cooked veal or chicken
1 (1 lb.) jar pickled beets, drained and chopped
1 cup diced dill pickles
¼ cup finely chopped onion
2 apples, peeled, cored and diced
2 hard cooked eggs, 1 chopped, 1 sliced
¼ cup mayonnaise
⅓ cup light cream
1 teaspoon pepper
1 tablespoon sugar
2 tomatoes, cut into wedges

In a large bowl, combine fish, meat, beets, pickles, onion, apples and the chopped egg. In a small bowl, blend mayonnaise, cream, pepper and sugar. Combine with fish mixture, place in refrigerator and let stand several hours to blend flavors. Arrange on individual salad plates or in a salad bowl, and garnish with egg slices and tomato wedges. Serve with bread sticks or fresh rolls.

Asparagus and chicken salad

Schwetzinger Spargelsalat

4 servings

4 tablespoons mayonnaise
1 teaspoon vinegar
1 tablespoon parsley flakes
½ teaspoon salt
½ teaspoon sugar
1½ cups cold, cubed, cooked chicken
1 cup pineapple chunks, drained
2 tomatoes, seeded and diced
2 (8½ oz.) cans asparagus pieces, drained

Combine mayonnaise, vinegar, parsley, salt and sugar; mix lightly; let stand 5–10 minutes. Combine chicken, pineapple and tomatoes in bowl. Add dressing mix; toss lightly. Arrange half the asparagus in salad bowl; pile chicken mix on top. Garnish with remaining asparagus.

Schwetzing molded eggs

Schwetzinger Eiergericht

4 servings

4 cooked asparagus tips, cut into 1″ pieces
4 eggs
½ teaspoon salt
⅛ teaspoon pepper
⅛ teaspoon paprika
2 tablespoons water
2 tablespoons melted margarine or butter

Place 4 asparagus pieces into each of 4 greased custard cups. Beat eggs with salt, pepper, paprika and water. Pour into prepared custard cups. Carefully pour melted margarine on surface of egg mixture. Place cups in a skillet. Pour boiling water into the pan to a depth of 1″ on the custard cups. Cover and heat in hot water (do not let water boil) until egg mixture is firm, about 20–30 minutes. When sharp knife is inserted in center and comes out clean, custards are done. Serve hot or cold, unmolded from custard cups.

Potato salad

Kartoffelsalat

6 servings

1 cup sour cream
½ cup mayonnaise
1 onion, finely chopped
1 tablespoon vinegar
1 tablespoon prepared mustard
2–3 teaspoons salt
1 teaspoon sugar
⅛ teaspoon black pepper
2 pounds small white potatoes
1 small cucumber, peeled and chopped
8 radishes, sliced
2 carrots, grated
2 hard cooked eggs, sliced
1 tomato, sliced
Chopped parsley

Combine sour cream, mayonnaise, onion, vinegar, mustard, salt, sugar and pepper; let stand 10–15 minutes. Cook unpeeled potatoes in boiling water until fork-tender about 20–25 minutes. Peel; cut into thin slices. Combine potatoes, cucumber, radishes and carrots in large bowl. Add sour cream mixture; toss lightly. Garnish with eggs, tomato and parsley. Salad may be served hot or cold.

Salted herring and beet salad

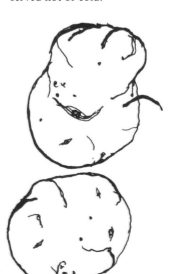

Rhenish Christmas salad

Rheinischer Weihnachtssalat

6 servings

> 3 cups cold cooked potatoes, cubed
> 2 cups diced apples
> ½ cup finely chopped onion
> 1 cup cold roast veal or chicken
> ¼ pound cubed ham or pork roll
> ½ cup cubed sour pickles
> 1 pickled herring fillet, cubed
> ¼ cup walnuts, coarsely chopped
> ¾ cup water
> 1 tablespoon vinegar
> 1 teaspoon salt
> 1 teaspoon sugar
> ½ cup mayonnaise
> 1 cup sour cream
> 2 hard-cooked eggs, sliced
> Chopped parsley

Combine potatoes, apples, onion, veal, ham, pickles, herring and walnuts in a large bowl; toss lightly. Sprinkle with water, vinegar, salt and sugar; blend well. Stir together mayonnaise and sour cream; blend into potato mixture. Chill. Serve garnished with egg slices and chopped parsley.

Mushroom salad

Champignons Salat

6 servings

> 1 pound fresh mushrooms, sliced
> 4 sweet gherkin pickles, finely chopped
> 2 tablespoons minced onion
> 1 clove garlic, minced
> 1 tomato, finely chopped
> ½ cup salad oil
> ¼ cup vinegar
> ½ teaspoon sugar
> 6 lettuce cups

Combine mushrooms, pickles onion, garlic and tomato; toss lightly. Add oil, vinegar and sugar; toss lightly until mushrooms are well coated. Chill at least 2 hours. Serve in lettuce cups.

Bremen salad

Bremer Salat

4 servings

> ½ cup sour cream
> ¼ cup mayonnaise
> ½ teaspoon curry powder
> 1 (5 oz.) jar pickled herring, diced
> ¼ pound bologna, diced
> 1 apple, peeled, cored and diced
> 2 stalks celery, diced
> 1 dill pickle, diced
> Lettuce

Combine sour cream, mayonnaise and curry powder; blend well. Let stand 5–10 minutes. Add remaining ingredients; toss lightly. Chill. Serve on lettuce.

Herring in sour cream

Hering in saurer Sahne

4 servings

> 1 cup sour cream
> 2 tablespoons vinegar
> ½ teaspoon sugar
> 1 medium onion, cut into rings
> 2 (5 oz.) jars herring in wine sauce, drained

Combine sour cream, vinegar and sugar; blend well. Add onion. Arrange herring on serving dishes. Spoon sour cream mixture over herring.

Cheese sandwich

Käse Schnitte

6 servings

1 large onion, finely chopped
2 teaspoons salad oil
1 teaspoon vinegar
¼ teaspoon salt
6 slices pumpernickel bread
Margarine or butter
Limburger or cream cheese
Freshly ground black pepper

Combine onion, oil vinegar and salt; let stand 10 minutes. Spread bread generously with margarine, then cheese. Spoon onion mixture over cheese; sprinkle with pepper.

Cold roast sandwiches

Hamburger Rundstück

4 open-faced sandwiches

2 tablespoons mayonnaise
1 tablespoon yogurt
2 tablespoons fresh chopped herbs (parsley, chives, savory) or 2 teaspoons mixed dried herbs
Salt, to taste
Pepper, to taste
4 slices bread, toasted and buttered, if desired
4 lettuce leaves
8 thin slices cold roast veal or pork
Crabapples
Parsley

Combine mayonnaise, yogurt, and herbs. Season with salt and pepper. Chill. Arrange lettuce leaves on toast. Top with 2 slices trimmed roast pork or veal on each slice. Spread sauce on meat. Cut in half. Garnish with crabapples and parsley.

Büsum slices

Büsumer Schnittchen

4 servings

4 eggs
½ teaspoon salt
¼ teaspoon paprika
2 tablespoons chopped chives
2 tablespoons margarine or butter
1 medium onion, chopped
1 (4½-oz.) can shrimp
4 slices buttered rye or pumpernickel bread, toasted
4 dill gherkin slices
4 tomato slices

Beat together eggs, salt, paprika, and chives. Melt margarine in skillet. Add onions and cook until transparent. Stir in shrimp and cook until heated. Pour egg mixture over onion and shrimp; scramble, stirring slowly. Serve on toast while still warm. Garnish with dill gherkin and tomato slices

Sausage and onion salad

Wurstsalat

4 servings

4 tablespoons oil
5 teaspoons vinegar
1 teaspoon sugar
½ teaspoon salt
⅛ teaspoon black pepper
½ pound bologna or luncheon meat, thinly sliced
2 dill pickles, chopped
2 stalks celery, chopped
1 medium onion, cut into rings
1 green pepper, chopped
1 cup cooked peas
Lettuce leaves

Combine oil, vinegar, sugar, salt and black pepper in small jar; shake well to blend. Combine meat, pickles, celery, onion, green pepper and peas; toss lightly. Add dressing; toss lightly. Chill at least 20 minutes. Serve on lettuce leaves.

Sausage and onion salad

Sauces

Mustard is so important to German cooking that many sauces use it as a base. Mustard is the best friend of pork, and given the immense popularity of pork products in Germany, the mustard pot is almost always on the table.

Mustard is an ancient herb. The Roman legions took it with them throughout Europe. Under the primitive conditions of Europe's Dark Ages, where many of the arts of civilization had been lost, mustard was very popular for preserving the freshness of meat and fish.

Basically, mustard consists of seeds from the mustard plant, which are ground to a fine powder (in the old days with a large stone crusher) and mixed with vinegar and spices. Mustard used to be prepared with sour grape juice, hence the name 'most', meaning unfermented grapejuice.

There are many different varieties of mustard in Germany, some stronger than others, some prepared with wine vinegar, some with beer vinegar and some with fresh green herbs. For fish the Germans use a very light mustard, made from white mustard seeds, and a somewhat darker mustard is used to accompany beer sausages.

Mustard is also used in German cooking to give certain sauces more body and in the preparation of braised meat and game. Meat that has been rubbed with mustard becomes deliciously tender when braised: the sharp flavor of the mustard disappears and only the aroma remains.

Medium mustard sauce

Senfsauce

Makes 2 cups

    4 tablespoons margarine or
      butter
    4 tablespoons flour
1–2 tablespoons dry mustard
    1 teaspoon sugar
    2 cups beef bouillon

Melt margarine in saucepan over low heat. Add flour, mustard and sugar; stir until blended smooth. Slowly add bouillon, stirring constantly to avoid lumps. Cook, stirring until smooth and thickened. For thick sauce increase flour to ½ cup.

Bacon sauce

Specksauce

Makes 2 cups

½ pound lean bacon, diced
 1 medium onion, chopped
 5 tablespoons flour
 2 cups beef bouillon
 1 teaspoon vinegar

Fry out bacon in heavy saucepan. Add onion; cook until onion is transparent. Drain off fat; return 2 tablespoons to saucepan. Add flour; stir until blended smooth. Slowly add bouillon and vinegar, stirring constantly to avoid lumps. Cook, stirring until smooth and thickened.

Horseradish and bread sauce

Semmelkren

Makes 2 cups

  2 cups beef bouillon
½ cup prepared horseradish
  2 slices white bread, crusts removed and cubed
  1 tablespoon cornstarch
  2 tablespoons water
½ cup light cream
½ cup sour cream

Combine bouillon, horseradish and bread in saucepan; bring to a boil. Reduce heat; simmer 5–8 minutes or until bread dissolves. Mix cornstarch and water; stir into bouillon mixture. Cook, stirring constantly, until thickened. Stir in cream and sour cream; heat.

Herb sauce

Frankfurter grüne Sauce

Makes 1 cup

  1 (8 oz.) **carton** plain yogurt, chilled
¼ cup mayonnaise
½ teaspoon dill weed
½ teaspoon dried chervil
½ teaspoon parsley flakes
½ teaspoon chives
¼ teaspoon salt
⅛ teaspoon black pepper
  2 hard cooked eggs, chopped

Combine yogurt, mayonnaise and seasonings; blend well. Stir in chopped egg.

South German salad dressing

Süddeutscher Salat

Makes ½ cup

  1 small onion, quartered
  2 tablespoons chopped parsley
  2 tablespoons chopped chives
  2 tablespoons boiling water
  2 tablespoons vinegar
  4 tablespoons salad oil
  1 teaspoon prepared mustard
½ teaspoon salt
¼ teaspoon black pepper

Combine all ingredients in blender jar; blend smooth.

Cold chive sauce

Kalte Schnittlauchsauce

Makes 1 cup

  2 (3 oz.) packages cream cheese and chives
  2 teaspoons chives
¼ teaspoon salt
  Dash black pepper
¼ cup milk

Cream together cheese, chives, salt and pepper. Gradually stir in milk; blend until smooth.

Soups

The word soup is linguistically linked with the German word 'saufen', meaning to drink abundantly. Which may help to explain why every German loves soup and no German lunch is complete without it. There is a soup for every occasion and practically every day of the year in Germany. Germany has a continental climate with fairly cold winters. A snowy day calls for a hearty, well-seasoned soup, preferably made with peas or beans, with a thick pig's foot and a variety of herbs. The glass of beer that follows tastes as good as it ever will. If something more filling is required there is a soup with 'Knödel', which are dumplings made with flour and sometimes blended with ground liver.

But if soup is just the beginning of a long festive dinner (and on must be careful not to spoil the appetite for the good things still to come) then a delicious 'Fleischbrühe' is ladled out. This is a tasty, clear broth prepared very slowly from meat and bones and then richly seasoned with fresh garden herbs. On a hot summer's day the Germans make a delicous cold fruit soup from cherries that quenches all thirst and conquers all lethargy.

**Liver dumpling soup—
see recipe page 35**

Liver dumpling soup. Eating a bowl of soup with a large slippery dumpling in it requires just a little bit of caution. The most practical way to proceed is to carefully break the dumpling up with your spoon and then stir it into the soup.

Liver dumpling soup

Leberknödelsuppe

4 servings

- ¼ pound beef liver
- 1 egg
- 2 tablespoons melted margarine or butter
- ¾ cup fine bread crumbs
- 1 small onion, finely chopped
- 1 teaspoon parsley flakes
- ¼ teaspoon dried marjoram
- ¼ teaspoon salt
- 4 cups beef bouillon

Remove membranes from liver. Mince finely or chop in blender. Combine liver, egg, margarine, bread crumbs, parsley, marjoram and salt; mix well. Chill about 25–30 minutes. Bring bouillon to a boil. Form meat mixture into 4 meatballs. Drop meatballs into simmering bouillon. Cook 10 minutes. Serve meatballs with bouillon in large soup bowls.

Beer soup

Biersuppe

4 servings

- 2 cups milk
- 1 stick cinnamon
- 1 piece lemon peel, 1" wide
- 1 tablespoon sugar
- 2 tablespoons cornstarch
- ¼ cup cold water
- 1 (12 oz.) can beer
- 1 egg yolk, slightly beaten

In saucepan, combine milk, cinnamon, lemon peel and sugar; bring to a boil. Reduce heat; simmer 10 minutes. Dissolve cornstarch in cold water; stir into milk mixture. Continue to cook, stirring constantly, until thickened. Stir in beer; heat. Beat a small amount of hot beer mixture into egg; return to saucepan. Stir well. Remove from heat; strain. Serve hot or cold.

Hamburg cold cherry soup

Hamburger Kirschkaltschale

6–8 servings

- 2 (16 oz.) cans sour pitted cherries in water
- 1 cup sugar
- 1 stick cinnamon
- 1 tablespoon cornstarch
- 2 tablespoons water
  Crushed macaroons, optional

Combine cherries and liquid, sugar, and cinnamon in saucepan; stir well. Bring to a boil; reduce heat; simmer 10 minutes. Press through fine sieve; return to saucepan; heat. Dissolve cornstarch in cold water; stir into hot mixture. Continue to cook, stirring constantly, until thickened. Serve hot or well chilled. Sprinkle with crushed macaroons before serving.

Shrimp bisque

Krabben Bisque

4 servings

- 2 (10½ oz.) cans cream of shrimp soup
- 1 soup can milk
- ½ pound shrimp, shelled and cleaned
- ¼ teaspoon fennel seed, crushed
- ¼ teaspoon dill weed
- 1 cup heavy cream

Combine soup and milk in saucepan; stir until well blended. Add shrimp, fennel and dill. Cook over medium heat, stirring constantly, until heated. Slowly stir in cream; heat. Serve immediately.

Baden leek soup—see recipe page 37

A good leek soup is made by using not only the white part of the leek, but also the tender yellow-green part.

Baden leek soup

Badische Lauchsuppe

6–8 servings

- 4 *leeks*
- ½ *cup margarine or butter*
- 2 *large onions, chopped*
- 6 *cups water*
- 6 *chicken bouillon cubes*
- ½ *teaspoon salt*
- 1 *cup milk*
- 1 *cup finely chopped ham, optional*

Slice leeks lengthwise; wash thoroughly under running water; cut into 1″ pieces. Melt margarine in heavy saucepan; sauté leeks and onions until leeks are soft. Add water, bouillon cubes, and salt. Bring to a boil; reduce heat; simmer 8–10 minutes, stirring occasionally. Add milk; heat. Ladle soup into serving dishes; sprinkle with chopped ham.

Buttermilk soup

Buttermilchsuppe

4–6 servings

- 3 *tablespoons cornstarch*
- 4 *cups buttermilk*
- 1 *tablespoon chives*
- 1 *teaspoon salt*
- 1 *egg yolk*
- 1 *hard cooked egg, chopped*

Stir cornstarch into buttermilk until smooth. Cook over medium heat, stirring constantly, until thick. Stir in salt and chives. Beat a small amount of hot mixture into egg; return to buttermilk mixture; stir well. Serve hot. Garnish with chopped egg.

East Prussian bread soup

Ostpreußische Brotsuppe

4 servings

- 8 *slices white bread, crusts removed and cubed*
- 4 *cups water*
- 4 *cloves*
- 1 *stick cinnamon*
- 1 *tablespoon sugar*
- ½ *teaspoon salt*
- ½ *cup sour cream*
- 1 *tablespoon lemon juice*

Combine bread, water, cloves, cinnamon, sugar and salt in saucepan. Bring to a boil; reduce heat; simmer 15 minutes. Strain. Heat; stir in sour cream and lemon juice.

Nurnberg vegetable soup

Nürnberger Gemüsesuppe

6 servings

- 2 *(10¾ oz.) cans vegetable soup with beef*
- 1 *(10½ oz.) can beef bouillon*
- 1 *soup can water*
- 1 *teaspoon dried chervil*
- ¼ *cup sour cream*

Combine soup, bouillon, water and chervil in saucepan. Bring to a boil; reduce heat. Stir in sour cream. Serve.

Westerland fish soup—see recipe page 39

This hearty Westerland fish soup with bread is a complete meal in itself.

Westerland fish soup

Westerländer Fischsuppe

6–8 servings

- ¼ cup margarine or butter
- 4 medium onions, chopped
- 2 (1 lb.) packages frozen fish fillets, cut into bite size pieces
- 2 medium potatoes, cubed
- 4 cups water
- 2 (8 oz.) bottles clam juice
- 4 tomatoes, peeled and quartered
- 1 cup broad noodles
- ¼ cup cooked diced bacon, drained
- ¼ pound shrimp, shelled and cleaned
- 1 small cucumber, peeled and chopped
- 1 teaspoon parsley flakes
- 1 pound mussels or clams, in shells

Melt margarine in large heavy saucepan. Sauté onions until transparent. Add fish, potatoes and water. Bring to a boil; reduce heat; simmer 15 minutes. Add clam juice, tomatoes and noodles; simmer 8–10 minutes. Stir in bacon, shrimp, cucumber and parsley. Add mussels. Cook just until mussel shells open.

Oxtail soup

Ochsenschwanzsuppe

6–8 servings

- 2 pounds oxtails, well trimmed
- 2 medium onions, cut into wedges
- 1 large carrot, quartered
- 2 cups celery tops, about 3" pieces
- 1 teaspoon salt
- ¼ teaspoon pepper
- 4 cloves or allspice berries
- 2 quarts water
- 1 carrot, peeled and diced
- 1 parsnip or small turnip, peeled and diced
- 2 slices boiled ham, diced
- 2 cups fine noodles, lightly packed

Place oxtails, onion, quartered carrot, celery, salt, pepper, cloves, and water in large kettle. Cover. Bring to a boil; reduce heat; simmer about 4 hours or until meat is loosened from bones. Strain; discard vegetables. Remove meat from bones; dice. Measure liquid; add water to make 8 cups. Bring to a boil; add diced carrots and parsnips; boil about 10 minutes. Add oxtail meat, ham and noodles. Cook until noodles are just tender, about 5 minutes.

Mussel chowder

Muschelsuppe

4 servings

- 2 pounds mussels or clams in shell
- ¼ cup water
- 3 slices bacon, diced
- 2 medium onions, chopped
- 1 stalk celery, chopped
- 3 medium potatoes, peeled and cubed
- 1 teaspoon salt
- ⅛ teaspoon black pepper
- 2 cups milk
  Margarine or butter

Wash and scrub mussels. Place mussels in large saucepot with the water. Cook just until shells open. Strain; reserve liquid. Remove mussels from shells and chop coarsely. In heavy saucepot fry out bacon. Sauté onions and celery until onions are transparent. Add potatoes, salt, pepper and 1 cup mussel broth. Cook until potatoes are tender about 15–20 minutes. Stir in milk and mussels; heat. Top each serving of chowder with a generous pat of margarine.

Potato soup

Kartoffelsuppe

4–6 servings

- 2 (10-½ oz.) cans chicken consommé
- 1 soup can water
- 2 cups diced potatoes
- 2 scallions, chopped
- 1 soup can milk
- 1 teaspoon Worcestershire sauce
- ½ cup sour cream

Combine consommé, water, potatoes and scallions in large saucepan; bring to a boil. Reduce heat; simmer until potatoes are tender, about 12 minutes. Blend smooth in blender or press through fine sieve; return to saucepan. Stir in milk and Worcestershire sauce; heat. Stir in sour cream. Serve hot or well chilled.

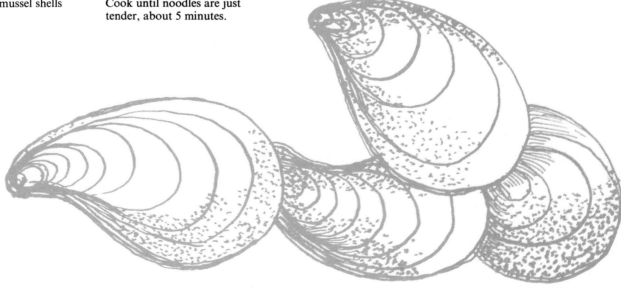

Red wine soup

Pfälzer Rotweinsuppe

4 servings

> 2 cups dry red wine
> 2 cups water
> 4 tablespoons minute tapioca
> 2 tablespoons sugar
> ½ stick cinnamon
> 1 piece lemon peel, ½" thick
> 2 egg whites
> 1 tablespoon sugar
>   Ladyfingers or sweet wafers

Combine wine, water, tapioca, sugar, cinnamon and lemon peel in saucepan. Bring to a boil; reduce heat; simmer 8–10 minutes, stirring frequently. Beat egg whites until soft peaks form. Gradually beat in sugar; beating until stiff. Strain soup. Top each serving of soup with "icebergs" of egg white. Serve hot.

The Pfalz region is the great wine cellar of Germany and, of course, the region where you would expect them to know how to make a good wine soup.

Fish stew Büsum style—see recipe page 42

Fish stew Büsum style. Grated horseradish is a natural partner of freshwater fish soups because the fish is somewhat bland and needs a little perking up.

Fish stew Büsum style

Büsumer Fischsuppe

6–8 servings

4 medium onions, sliced
1 stalk celery, chopped
2 (1 lb.) packages frozen
    perch fillets, cut into
    serving size pieces
1 tablespoon salt
2 tablespoons margarine or
    butter
5 cups milk
½ cup sour cream
2 tablespoons chopped
    dill pickle
4 teaspoons horseradish
1 teaspoon parsley flakes
    Fresh chopped dill

Place onions, celery, fish, salt
and margarine in large heavy
saucepan; add milk. Bring to a
boil; reduce heat; simmer
15–20 minutes. Add sour
cream, pickle, horseradish and
parsley; stir to blend; heat.
Garnish with dill.

Hamburg fish casserole

Hamburger Kasserolle

6 servings

2 tablespoons margarine or
    butter
1 medium onion, chopped
1 (16 oz.) package frozen
    fish fillets, cut into
    bite-size pieces
½ pound scallops
½ pound shrimp, shelled and
    cleaned
1 (10 oz.) package frozen
    artichoke hearts, thawed
1 (3 oz.) can sliced
    mushrooms, drained
1 (10½ oz.) can mushroom
    soup

1 cup dry white wine
½ teaspoon salt
2 cups cooked rice
2 teaspoons parsley flakes
2 tablespoons grated Parmesan
    cheese

Melt margarine in large skillet;
sauté onion in margarine until
transparent. Add fish,
scallops, shrimp, artichoke
hearts, mushrooms, soup,
wine and salt; mix well.
Combine rice and parsley in
greased 2½ qt. casserole.
Pour fish mixture over rice.
Bake in a moderate oven (350°)
20 minutes. Sprinkle cheese
over top; bake 10 minutes
longer.

'Councellors' fish

Ratsherren-Fisch

4 servings

1½ pounds frozen fish fillets,
    thawed
½ teaspoon salt
¼ teaspoon black pepper
¼ cup margarine or butter,
    melted
¼ cup milk
1 tablespoon flour
⅔ cup grated cheddar cheese
1 tablespoon snipped parsley

Place fish fillets in buttered
shallow casserole (7″ × 10″).
Sprinkle with salt and pepper.
Pour melted margarine over
fillets. Bake in a hot oven
(400°) for 15–20 minutes or
until fish flakes when tested
with fork. Mix milk, flour, and
cheese together. Pour over
fillets and return them to
oven until top is browned,
about 10–12 minutes. Sprinkle
with parsley.

Hamburg fish casserole

*The fish casserole from Hamburg
is a rich dish, worthy of the
prosperous harbor city from
which it takes its name*

Poached fillets in dill sauce

Gedünste Fisch-Filets in Dillsauce

4 servings

1½ cups water
1 teaspoon salt
1 medium onion, sliced
1 bay leaf
1 (16 oz.) package frozen
  fish fillets, thawed
2 tablespoons margarine or
  butter
2 tablespoons flour
½ cup sour cream
2 tablespoons fresh dill,
  chopped

In a large skillet, combine
water, salt, onion, and bay
leaf; bring to a boil. Turn
down heat so that water is
simmering. Carefully add fish
fillets. Poach for 8–10 minutes
or until fillets flake when tested
with a fork. Gently remove
fillets from pan; keep warm
on serving platter. Strain fish
broth and reserve 1 cup. In a
small saucepan, melt margarine.
Stir in flour; gradually add
fish broth, stirring constantly.
Cook until thickened. Remove
from heat and stir in sour
cream and dill. Serve sauce
over fillets.

Fish patties with sweet-sour sauce

Fish patties with sweet-sour sauce

Fischklopse in Specksauce

6 servings

1 cup croutons
¼ cup milk
1 pound cooked fish, ground
1 egg
1 tablespoon grated onion
½ teaspoon salt
1 cup fine bread crumbs
2 tablespoons margarine or
  butter
1 (10½ oz.) can cream of
  shrimp soup
½ cup milk
2 teaspoons vinegar

Soak croutons in milk until
soft; drain well. Combine
croutons, fish, egg, onion and
salt; mix well. Add ¼–½ cup
bread crumbs as needed to
make a firm mixture. Shape into
2″ × 1″ patties. Roll in
remaining bread crumbs.
Melt margarine in large skillet,
brown patties in margarine.
Combine soup, milk and vinegar
in saucepan; blend well. Heat.
Serve sauce over patties.

Pan-fried trout Starnberg style

Gebackene Forelle Starnberger Art

4 servings

- 4 trout, cleaned and pan-ready
- 2 teaspoons Worcestershire sauce
- 2 teaspoons salt
- 4 tablespoons flour
- 4 tablespoons salad oil
- 4 tablespoons margarine or butter
- 3 shallots, finely minced or 1 small onion, finely chopped
- 2 tablespoons lemon juice
- 1 teaspoon parsley flakes
- ½ teaspoon dried tarragon

Rub insides of fish with Worcestershire sauce, then with salt. Dredge fish with flour. Heat oil in large skillet. Fry fish in hot oil 3 minutes on each side. Remove fish; keep warm. Pour off oil. Melt margarine in skillet; stir in shallots, lemon juice, parsley, and tarragon; heat. Pour over fish.

Trout and white wine (Hock or Moselle) are a celebrated combination in good German cuisine.

Whole flounder, Hamburg style

Flunder, Hamburger Art

4 servings

½ pound bacon, diced
4 flounder (about 12 oz. each) cleaned, pan-ready
2 teaspoons lemon juice
1 teaspoon salt
¼ cup flour
¼ cup margarine or butter
  Parsley sprigs
  Lemon wedges

Fry diced bacon until crisp; drain on paper towels. Sprinkle each flounder with lemon juice and salt; coat with flour, shaking off excess. Melt margarine in large frying pan over moderately high heat. Fry fish slowly, about 5 minutes on each side, until golden brown. Arrange fish on platter, garnished with bacon pieces, parsley sprigs and lemon slices. Serve with potato sald.

Rhine salmon

Rheinsalm

4 servings

1 cup dry white wine
½ cup water
1 onion, quartered
1 bay leaf
½ teaspoon salt
4 salmon steaks, 1" thick
1 cup light cream
3 egg yolks, slightly beaten

Combine wine, water, onion, bay leaf and salt in large skillet. Bring to a boil; reduce heat. Place fish in skillet. Cover. Simmer until fish flakes easily when tested with a fork, about 10 minutes. Remove fish; keep warm. Discard bay leaf and onion. Boil mixture in skillet until reduced to 1 cup. Combine cream and eggs. Beat a small amount of hot broth into egg mixture; return to skillet. Continue to cook, stirring constantly, until thickened. Pour over salmon steaks.

Baked fish with caper sauce

Gebackener Fisch mit Kapernsauce

4 servings

1 (2 lb) pike or other fresh water fish
½ teaspoon salt
¼ cup margarine or butter, melted
3 tablespoons flour
2 cups hot fish or chicken bouillon
2 teaspoons capers
2 anchovy fillets, chopped
½ teaspoon sugar
2 tablespoons lemon juice

Clean fish and wash thoroughly in cold water. Sprinkle with salt. Place in buttered baking dish. Pour melted margarine over fish. Bake in a moderate oven (350°) for about 20–25 minutes, or until fish flakes when tested with a fork. Remove from baking dish; place on platter and keep warm. Sprinkle flour into remaining liquid in baking dish and stir to blend. Gradually add bouillon. Cook, stirring constantly, until thickened. Stir in capers, anchovies, sugar, and lemon juice. Serve sauce hot with baked fish.

Poached codfish

Friesischer Pfannfisch

4–6 servings

2 pounds fresh codfish fillet or steak
10 peppercorns, crushed
1 bay leaf
1 tablespoon chopped parsley
2 cups water
2 tablespoons margarine or butter
2 tablespoons cornstarch
1½ tablespoons lemon juice
  Salt and pepper
1½ pounds hot, cooked potatoes, cut into 1" cubes
  Chopped parsley

Place fish, peppercorns, bay leaf, parsley and water into a wide skillet or saucepan. Bring to the boiling point. (Do NOT allow to boil.) Poach until fish is tender, about 5–10 minutes. Carefully remove the fish to warm platter. Strain liquid, reserving 2 cups. Melt margarine in saucepan; blend in cornstarch. Gradually add the reserved fish stock. Cook over medium heat, stirring constantly, until thickened, about 3–5 minutes. Stir in lemon juice. Season to taste with salt and pepper. Stir in potato cubes. Serve the sauce with the fish, or break the fish into approximately 1" cubes and stir very gently into the sauce. Serve garnished with additional chopped parsley.

Trout from the numerous small brooks of Germany's mountains are considered a sort of national fish. The delicate taste is brought out best when the trout is poached and served with melted butter.

Poached trout

Gedünste Forelle

4 servings

    2 cups water
    1 tablespoon parsley flakes
    1 onion, quartered
    2 bay leaves
    3 cloves
    1 teaspoon salt
    4 trout, cleaned and pan-ready
    ½ cup melted margarine or
       butter
       Parsley sprigs
       Lemon wedge

Combine water, parsley, onion, bay leaves, cloves and salt in large skillet. Bring to a boil; add fish. Reduce heat; cover; simmer 12–15 minutes or until fish flakes easily when tested with a fork. Carefully remove fish to serving dish; pour over melted margarine. Garnish with parsley sprigs and lemon wedges.

Fish in beer, East Prussian style

Ostpreußische Bierfische

6 servings

- 2 cups water
- 1 (12 oz.) bottle dark beer
- 1 tablespoon finely chopped parsley
- ½ cup celery, chopped
- 1 medium onion, chopped
- 2 teaspoons salt
- 1 teaspoon pickling spice
- 1 teaspoon margarine or butter
- 3 pounds flounder fillet, carp or pike, cut into serving pieces
- 3 tablespoons cornstarch
- ¼ cup water
- 1 teaspoon lemon juice
  Sugar
  Parsley sprigs

Combine water, beer, parsley, celery, onion, salt, pickling spice, and margarine in large skillet or wide saucepan. Bring to boiling point; do not allow to boil. Add fish pieces. Poach until fish flakes easily when tested with fork, about 3–5 minutes, depending on thickness of pieces. Carefully remove fish to heated platter with slotted spoon. Strain broth. Combine cornstarch and water. Add to broth. Bring to a boil and cook until thickened, stirring constantly. Add lemon juice. Season to taste with a little sugar. Serve fish and sauce separately with boiled potatoes. Garnish with parsley sprigs.

Poached mackerel with herbs

Wriezener Makrelen

4 servings

- 4 whole mackerel, cleaned
- 1 tablespoon vinegar
- 1 teaspoon salt
- ¼ teaspoon black pepper
- 1 onion, quartered
- ½ cup water
- 1 cup white wine
- 3 peppercorns, crushed
- ½ bay leaf
- 1 whole clove
- ½ teaspoon thyme
- 2 tablespoons cornstarch
- ¼ cup water
- ½ cup cream
- 2 tablespoons margarine or butter
- 1½ tablespoons chopped chives
- 1½ tablespoons chopped parsley

Sprinkle fish with vinegar, salt, and pepper. In large skillet mix onion, water, wine, peppercorns, bay leaf, clove, and thyme; bring to a boil Carefully add fish; reduce heat and cover. Poach for 15–20 minutes or until fish flakes when tested with fork. Remove fish and keep warm. Strain fish broth; measure 1 cup. Return to skillet. Blend cornstarch into cold water; add fish broth. Cook until thickened and clear. Stir in cream, margarine, chives and parsley. Serve hot over fish.

Eel fricassee

Bremer Aalfrikassee

6 servings

- 1 tablespoon beef extract
- 3 (1-pt.) bottles clam broth
- 2 pounds fresh eel, cleaned, skinned and cut into 1½" pieces, or
- 1½ pounds red snapper or haddock fillet, cut into 1½" × 1" pieces

Fish balls:
- 2 onions, peeled and cut into 6 wedges each
- ½ pound haddock fillet
- 2 egg whites
- ½ cup half-and-half
- ½ teaspoon salt
- ⅛ teaspoon pepper

Sauce:
- 2 tablespoons margarine or butter
- 4 tablespoons flour
- 2 cups poaching liquid
- 2 egg yolks
- ½ cup half-and-half
- ½ cup dry white wine
- 1 (8 oz.) can sliced mushrooms, drained
- ½ pound frozen cooked, cleaned shrimp
- 1 (8 oz.) can cut asparagus pieces, drained

Combine beef extract and clam broth in large, wide skillet or saucepan. Add eel or other fish pieces. Poach for 15 minutes or until fish flakes easily when tested with fork. Carefully remove fish. Keep warm. Reserve 2 cups liquid. Put onions and haddock fillet through finest blade of food grinder. Beat in egg whites, half-and-half and salt and pepper. Form into 1" balls. Poach fish balls in hot, but not boiling water for about 10 minutes. Drain. Melt margarine in saucepan, stir in flour and reserved 2 cups broth; cook over medium heat, stirring constantly, until mixture thickens. Combine egg yolks with half-and-half; add small amount of the hot mixture, stirring well. Return to saucepan, stirring briskly. Stir in wine, mushrooms, shrimp and asparagus. Add reserved poached fish and fish balls. Blend carefully. Serve hot with rice and cucumber salad.

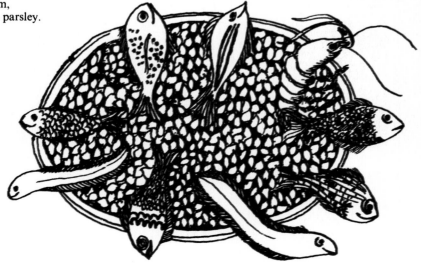

Meat Dishes

There is a droll German proverb that 'the most delicous vegetable in the world is meat' ...and another that 'in times of disaster sausages are eaten even without bread'.

Meat, as we can see, means quite a lot to the German diet, particularly in the form of 'Wurst' (sausage) which is the pillar of German cooking and is found in an almost endless variety of tastes: the light 'Weisswurst' from Munich, which is delicious with beer, the dark Thüringer Blutwurst (blood sausage), the hard Bierwurst, full-flavored Mettwurst, lightly sour Sülzle, spicy Kasseler or Berliner Leberwurst. They hang in the delicatessen in an appetizing and confusing array of colors and shapes: black, white, red and brown, hard and soft, long and short, thin and thick. At the wine feasts in Dürkheim and at the October beer festival in Munich, sausages are eaten by the million. For the great wine feast in Dürkheim alone, at least 200,000 liters of wine are poured out, and some 1000 oxen and 600 pigs disappear into the sausages.

Rhenish sauerbraten—see recipe page 49

With a German sauerbraten, you should always serve cooked, dried fruit.

Rhenish sauerbraten

Rheinischer Sauerbraten

6–8 servings

- 2 cups vinegar
- 2 cups water
- 4 onions, sliced
- 1 stalk celery, chopped
- 1 carrot, chopped
- 2 bay leaves
- 8 peppercorns, crushed
- 8 whole cloves
- ¼ teaspoon mustard seed
- 1 (4–5 lb.) rump roast of beef
- 1 teaspoon salt
- ¼ teaspoon pepper
- ¼ cup salad oil
- 4 tablespoons flour
- ½ cup seedless raisins
- ½ cup sour cream

Combine vinegar, water, onions, celery, carrot, bay leaves, peppercorns, cloves, and mustard seed in saucepan. Bring to a boil; cool. Place meat in large bowl. Pour marinade over meat. Place in refrigerator; marinate 2–3 days, turning several times. Remove meat from marinade; dry well. Sprinkle meat with salt and pepper. Heat oil in Dutch oven. Brown meat very well on all sides. Add 2 cups of the marinade; cover; simmer 2–3 hours or until meat is very tender. Remove meat; keep warm. Strain sauce; skim off fat; measure liquid. Add water or marinade to make 2 cups. Stir in flour. Return to pan. Cook over low heat, stirring and scraping browned bits, until thickened. Stir in raisins and sour cream; blend well. Serve with meat.

Braised stuffed beef rolls

Rindsrouladen

4 servings

- 8 very thin slices top beef round
- 1 medium onion, chopped
- ¼ pound bacon, diced
- ¼ cup flour
- 1 teaspoon paprika
- ½ teaspoon salt
- ½ teaspoon pepper
- 2 tablespoons salad oil
- 1 carrot, sliced
- 1 stalk celery, sliced
- 1 small onion or 1 leek, sliced
- ¼ cup coarsely cut parsley
- 1 cup hot water
- 1 tablespoon cornstarch
- 2 tablespoons cold water

Pound beef slices with mallet until very thin. Divide onion and bacon among the 8 beef slices, placing them across one end. Roll up with filling in center; secure rolls with toothpicks. Sprinkle all sides of rolls with flour, paprika, salt and pepper. In large skillet, brown in oil on all sides. Add carrot, celery, onion or leek and parsley; add hot water. Cover and simmer until tender, about 1½ to 2 hours, adding more water if needed. Remove rolls, remove toothpicks carefully and keep rolls warm. Strain and measure 1 cup liquid from skillet. Stir cornstarch into cold water; add to measured meat juices. Cook over medium heat, stirring constantly, until thickened. Serve with beef rolls.

Swabian fillet of beef

Schwäbischer Schlachtbraten

6 servings

- 1 (3–3½ lb.) beef tenderloin
- 1 large onion, chopped
- 1 stalk celery, chopped
- 1 carrot, chopped
- 4 tablespoons melted margarine or butter
- 1 cup beef bouillon
- 1 teaspoon flour
- 2 tablespoons dry white wine

Place meat on rack in roasting pan. Arrange vegetables around meat. Brush meat with melted butter. Insert meat thermometer into center of thickest part of meat. Roast in a very hot oven (450°), basting frequently, about 45–60 minutes or to 140° on thermometer. Remove meat; keep warm. Drain off fat, leaving brown bits in pan. Add bouillon to drippings in pan; scrape and stir until all brown bits are loosened. Mash vegetables with fork. Strain into saucepan. Stir in flour and wine; heat thoroughly. Serve over meat.

Pot roast with sour cream gravy

Schmorbraten mit saurer Sahnensauce

6–8 servings

- 2 tablespoons salad oil
- 1 (4–5 lb.) bottom round beef roast
- 1 medium onion, sliced
- 1 cup dry red wine
- 1 cup water
- 2 tablespoons flour
- ¼ cup cold water
- 1 teaspoon salt
- ¼ teaspoon black pepper
- ½ cup sour cream

Heat oil in Dutch oven; brown meat on all sides. Add onion, wine, and water. Cover and simmer gently for 3–4 hours or until tender. Remove meat and keep warm. Drain off all but 1½ cups liquid. Stir flour into cold water until blended; slowly stir into liquid in pan. Add salt and pepper. Cook, stirring, over low heat until thickened. Slowly blend in sour cream. Serve gravy with sliced pot roast.

Poached meatballs with lemon sauce

Königsberger Klopse

4 servings

   1 *pound ground beef*
   ½ *cup seasoned bread crumbs*
   1 *egg*
   1 *teaspoon grated lemon rind*
   1 *cup water*
   2 *beef bouillon cubes*
   1 *tablespoon lemon juice*
   1 *teaspoon cornstarch*
   2 *tablespoons cold water*
   1 *egg yolk*

Combine meat, bread crumbs, egg and lemon rind; mix lightly. Shape into 12 meatballs. Bring water to a boil in medium size saucepan; add bouillon cubes; stir until dissolved. Gently drop meatballs into simmering bouillon. Cook 8–10 minutes. Remove meatballs; keep warm. Add lemon juice to bouillon. Dissolve cornstarch in cold water; stir into hot bouillon. Continue to cook stirring constantly, until slightly thickened. Add a small amount of hot bouillon mixture to egg yolk; beat well; stir into hot bouillon. Remove from heat and pour over meatballs.

Poached meatballs with lemon sauce, the traditional dish of the old East-Prussian city of Königsberg. You can make it even more piquant by sprinkling on a few capers.

Silesian pork and dried fruit

Schlesisches Himmelreich

4–6 servings

  1 *tablespoon flour*
  2 *pounds boneless rolled pork*
  1 *cup dried apricots*
  1 cup dried apple slices
  1 *cup dried pitted prunes*
 ¼ *cup granulated brown sugar*
 ½ *cup dry white wine*

Dust the inside of a cooking bag with flour. Place meat and fruit in cooking bag; sprinkle with brown sugar. Pour wine over all. Tie bag securely. Puncture 4 small holes about 4″ apart in top of bag. Place bag in shallow roasting pan. Cook in a slow oven (325°) 1½ hours. Place meat on serving platter; arrange fruit around meat.

It is said that this typical East German dish owes its name 'Himmelreich' meaning Kingdom of Heaven, to the dried fruit that accompanies it.

Silesian fresh ham

Schlesischer Schwärtelbraten

8 servings

1 fresh ham (5–6 lb.)
1 teaspoon salt
½ teaspoon black pepper
1 teaspoon caraway seed
1 cup boiling water
1 medium onion, sliced
1 tablespoon cornstarch
¼ cup cold water
½ cup sour cream (optional)

Rub meat with salt. pepper,
and caraway seed. Place on
rack in roasting pan. Pour
water in bottom of roasting
pan; add onions. Roast in
moderate oven (350°) for 3–3½
hours or until a meat
thermometer reaches 185°.
Remove from pan and keep
warm. Pour off all but 3
tablespoons of fat.
Remove onions. Stir to loosen
drippings from pan, adding
water as necessary to increase
liquid to 1 cup. Mix cornstarch
with cold water. Add to gravy.
Cook over low heat, stirring
constantly, until thickened.
If desired, stir in sour cream.
Slice meat and serve with gravy.

Smothered pork chops

Geschmorte Schweinerippen

4 servings

4 pork chops, about ¾" thick
1 teaspoon salt
1 teaspoon dry mustard
1 tablespoon lemon juice
4 tablespoons margarine or
   butter
1 medium onion, chopped
1 (1 lb.) can whole, peeled
   tomatoes

Rub chops on both sides with
salt, mustard and lemon juice;
let stand for 30 minutes. Melt
margarine in skillet; brown
chops on both sides. Add
onions; let cook a few minutes
over medium heat until
transparent. Add tomatoes
with liquid. Cover and simmer
until tender, about 20–30
minutes. If sauce becomes too
thick or starts to separate, add
a few tablespoons hot water.
Serve immediately.

Smoked pork tenderloin with sauerkraut

Kasseler Rippchen mit Sauerkraut

4–6 servings

1 (2–3 lb.) smoked pork
   tenderloin or 1 smoked
   pork butt
1 (16 oz.) can sauerkraut
1 tablespoon minced onion
1 teaspoon caraway seed

Prepare the tenderloin according
to directions on package.
Cut into ½" slices. Mix together
sauerkraut, onion, and caraway
seed. Spread sauerkraut
mixture over the bottom of a
large casserole dish. Top with
tenderloin slices. Bake in a
moderate oven (350°) for
15–20 minutes or until
sauerkraut is heated.

Smoked loin of pork

Kasseler Rippenspeer

6–8 servings

1 (4–5 lb.) smoked loin of
   pork
¼ teaspoon black pepper
1 medium onion, sliced
1 cup hot water
1 cup dry red wine
   Braised sauerkraut page 49

Place meat in shallow roasting
pan; sprinkle with pepper;
add onion. Pour hot water over
meat. Roast in a hot oven
(400°) 30 minutes. Pour half the
wine over meat. Continue to
roast, basting frequently with
remaining wine, about 30
minutes or until meat is well
browned. Serve with braised
sauerkraut.

*Smoked loin of pork. That
delicious cooking smell that fills
German houses in the wintertime
is the unmistakable evidence of
sauerkraut being prepared with
smoked pork.*

Bavarian roast veal or pork

Bayerische Haxen

6 servings

- 1 (4 lb.) rump of veal or
  1 (3 lb.) boneless pork
  shoulder roll
- 1 teaspoon salt
- ½ cup boiling water
- 1 large onion, thinly sliced
- 1 carrot, chopped
- 3 peppercorns, crushed
- ½ teaspoon caraway seed

Place meat in roasting pan. Sprinkle with salt. Pour boiling water into pan. Add vegetables, peppercorns and caraway seed. Roast in a moderate oven (350°) until meat tests done on a meat thermometer, veal 170°; pork 185°, about 1 hour, 45 minutes. Baste with pan juices during roasting, adding more water if needed.

Fake wild boar

Falscher Wildschweinbraten

6–8 servings

- 3 pounds boneless rolled pork
- 10 juniper berries, crushed
- 2 teaspoons salt
- 1 teaspoon black pepper
- 4 tablespoons salad oil
- ½ cup dry red wine
- ¼ cup water
- ½ cup sour cream
- 1 tablespoon flour
- 1 tablespoon red currant jelly

Rub meat with juniper berries, salt and pepper; let stand 15–20 minutes. Heat oil in Dutch oven; brown meat on all sides. Add wine and water; cover; simmer about 1 hour. Remove meat; keep warm. Drain off excess fat. Combine sour cream, flour and jelly; stir into drippings. Cook over low heat, stirring constantly until slightly thickened and smooth. Serve with meat.

Creamed veal cutlets with dumplings

Rahmschnitzel mit Spätzle

4 servings

- 1 pound (4) veal cutlets
- ½ teaspoon salt
- ⅛ teaspoon black pepper
- 4 tablespoons margarine or butter
- 2 tablespoons chopped chives
- 1 teaspoon parsley flakes
- ½ cup dry white wine
- 1 tablespoon flour
- ½ cup sour cream
- *1 recipe Tiny dumplings, page 71. or hot cooked noodles*

Sprinkle cutlets with salt and pepper. Melt margarine in large skillet. Brown cutlets in margarine. Add chives, parsley and wine. Cover. Simmer 20–25 minutes. Remove cutlets; keep warm. Blend in flour. Cook, stirring constantly, until slightly thickened. Stir in sour cream; heat thoroughly, pour over veal. Serve with **dumplings** or noodles.

Braised sausage

Bratwurst

4 servings

- 1½ pounds link sausages
- ¼ cup fine dry bread crumbs
- 4 tablespoons margarine or butter
- ½ cup chopped onion
- 1 tablespoon flour
- 1 cup water
- 1 tablespoon tomato sauce
- ¼ teaspoon salt
- ¼ teaspoon thyme

Place sausages in large skillet, in one layer; just cover with hot water. Simmer 1–2 minutes until sausages are no longer pink. (Be sure sausages are cooked to center). Discard water. Drain on paper towels. Roll sausages in bread crumbs, coating well. Heat margarine in same skillet until quite hot. Place sausages in skillet; prick with a sharp-tined fork. Brown on all sides over moderate heat. Remove from pan and keep warm. Cook onion in fat remaining in pan over low heat until onion is transparent. Stir in flour, gradually add water and cook over medium heat, stirring frequently, until thickened, about 1 minute. Stir in tomato sauce. Season with salt to taste. Stir in thyme Serve gravy over sausages with mashed potatoes.

Creamed veal cutlets with dumplings

Kidneys Stuttgart style

Nieren Stuttgarter Art

4 servings

1½ pounds beef kidneys
2 tablespoons flour
1 teaspoon salt
¼ teaspoon black pepper
2 medium onions, sliced
¼ cup margarine or butter
1 cup beef bouillon
2 tablespoons lemon juice
¼ cup chopped parsley
⅓ cup cream or evaporated
 milk
2 tablespoons white wine
 (optional)
1 teaspoon paprika
1 tablespoon chopped chives

Soak kidneys in lightly salted water for about 1–2 hours. Slice and remove white membranes. Dry well. Dredge with flour seasoned with salt and pepper. Melt margarine in skillet and sauté onions until golden. Remove from pan. Sauté kidney slices until lightly browned. Add onions, bouillon, lemon juice, and parsley. Stir in cream or evaporated milk, and wine. Simmer for 5 minutes. Sprinkle with paprika and chives. Serve with rice.

Tongue with raisin sauce

Weimarer Ochsenzunge

8 servings

1 pre-cooked beef tongue
 (3–4 lbs.)
 Water to cover
1 onion, sliced
1 celery stalk
1 sprig of parsley
2 tablespoons margarine or
 butter
2 tablespoons flour
½ teaspoon salt
2 tablespoons vinegar
2 tablespoons sugar
⅔ cup raisins

Place tongue in deep saucepan with any juices packed with tongue; add water to cover. Add onion, celery, and parsley. Heat thoroughly; remove tongue and keep warm. Strain liquid and reserve 1½ cups. Melt margarine in saucepan; stir in flour and salt; slowly add the reserved cooking fluid. Stir until smooth and thickened; stir in vinegar, sugar, and raisins. Continue to cook until well heated. Serve with sliced tongue.

Stuffed breast of veal

Gefüllte Kalbsbrust

4–6 servings

1 (3 ½ lb.) breast of veal with
 pocket for stuffing
½ teaspoon salt
⅛ teaspoon black pepper
¾ cup finely chopped onion
2 tablespoons chopped parsley
4 slices day old bread, cubed
2 tablespoons half-and-half
2 tablespoons salad oil
2 eggs
½ teaspoon paprika
½ teaspoon salt
 Dash black pepper
¼ cup margarine or butter
½ cup water
1 tablespoon cornstarch
¼ cup currant jelly
1 teaspoon lemon juice

Sprinkle inside pocket and outside of veal with salt and pepper. Mix together onion, parsley, bread cubes, half-and-half, oil, eggs, paprika, salt and pepper. Fill pocket with bread mixture; skewer shut. Melt margarine in Dutch oven. Place meat in margarine; add water. Cover. Cook over medium heat until veal is tender when pierced with a fork, about 1½ hours. Turn meat once after 45 minutes. Remove veal; keep warm. Measure any liquid in pan; add water to make 1 cup. Stir in cornstarch; return to pan. Cook over medium heat, stirring and scraping up browned bits, until thickened. Add jelly and lemon juice; stir until jelly is dissolved. Serve with veal.

Stuffed breast of veal

A typical German Sunday dish: stuffed breast of veal, thickly sliced, with a delicious, slightly sour sauce of currant jelly and lemon juice.

Westphalian leg of lamb

Westfälische Hammelkeule

4–6 servings

- 1 small onion, chopped
- 1 carrot, chopped
- 1 tablespoon chopped parsley
- 2 tablespoons margarine or butter
- 1 bay leaf
- 1 (8 oz.) container plain yogurt or
- 1 cup buttermilk
- 1 tablespoon flour
- ½ leg of lamb (about 3½ lbs.)
- 1 teaspoon salt
- ⅛ teaspoon pepper
- 1 tablespoon cornstarch
- 2 tablespoons cold water

Sauté onion, carrot and parsley in margarine until onion is transparent. Add bay leaf and yogurt. Sprinkle flour in cooking bag large enough to contain the lamb. Place half of the yogurt mixture in the bag. Sprinkle lamb with salt and pepper. Place in bag on the yogurt mixture. Cover lamb with remaining mixture. Seal bag with twist tie. Puncture bag in 3 or 4 places with a 2-tined fork. Insert meat thermometer into the thickest part of the meat. Roast in a moderate oven (350°) until lamb registers 165° for medium or 180° for well-done. Carefully strain liquid from bag. Measure and make up to 1 cup with water, if necessary. Stir cornstarch into cold water. Add to liquid; cook over medium heat until thickened, stirring constantly. Taste, season with salt and pepper. Serve sauce with sliced lamb.

Sailors' stew

Bremer Matrosenfleisch

6 servings

- 2 tablespoons salad oil
- 1 pound beef, cut into 1" cubes
- 1 pound pork, cut into 1" cubes
- 2 medium onions, finely chopped
- 2 carrots, chopped
- 2 stalks celery, chopped
- 1 teaspoon salt
- ⅛ teaspoon black pepper
- 1 bay leaf
- 1 cup dry red wine
- 1 teaspoon cornstarch
- ¼ cup water
- 2 teaspoons horseradish

Heat oil in large Dutch oven. Brown meat on all sides. Add vegetables, salt, pepper, bay leaf and wine. Bring to a boil. Cover. Reduce heat; simmer 45–50 minutes. Discard bay leaf. Dissolve cornstarch in water; add horseradish. Stir into beef mixture. Continue to cook, stirring constantly, until slightly thickened.

Liver with mushrooms and white wine

Geschnetzelte Leber

4 servings

- 4 slices bacon, diced
- ¼ cup finely chopped onion
- 1 (6 oz.) package frozen sliced mushrooms
- 1 pound sliced baby beef liver, about 4 slices
- 1 tablespoon flour
- ½ teaspoon salt
  Dash black pepper
- ½ cup dry white wine
- 1 cup half-and-half or light cream
- 1 tablespoon chopped parsley

In large frying pan over moderate heat, fry bacon until crisp. Remove bacon pieces, drain and reserve. Add chopped onion and mushrooms to bacon fat in pan. Cook over medium heat until onions are transparent. Remove skins and tubes from liver; cut into ¼" × ½" × 2" strips. Add to hot fat and toss to brown, 3–4 minutes. Sprinkle flour, salt and pepper over liver. Stir to blend. Stir in wine, then half-and-half. Heat to a boil; reduce heat and simmer 4–5 minutes. Serve garnished with parsley and reserved bacon pieces. Serve with rice or **Tiny dumplings, page 49.**

Liver with mushrooms and white wine

56

Liver and apples, Berlin style

Berliner Leber

4 servings

- 1 pound beef liver, cut into 4 slices
- ½ teaspoon salt
- ⅛ teaspoon black pepper
- ¼ cup margarine or butter
- 1 large onion, cut into thick slices (optional)
- 2 apples, peeled, cored and cut into thick slices

Sprinkle liver with salt and pepper. Melt margarine in large skillet. Cook liver slices in margarine about 3 minutes each side. Remove; keep warm. Add onion and apple slices to skillet; cook, turning frequently, until onions are lightly browned. Serve over liver.

Berlin style chicken fricassee—see recipe page 58

Berlin style chicken fricassee

Berliner Hühnerfrikassee

6 servings

> 2 (8 oz.) cans chicken gravy
> 4 tablespoons dry white wine
> 1 tablespoon lemon juice
> 2 cups cubed, cooked chicken
> 1 cup diced ham
> 6 sausages, cooked and sliced
> 1 (3 oz.) can sliced
>   mushrooms, drained
> 1 tablespoon capers
> 1 (8½ oz.) can asparagus
>   pieces, drained
> ½ cup sour cream
>   **Tiny dumplings**

Combine gravy, wine and lemon juice in saucepan; blend well. Stir in chicken, ham, sausages and mushrooms. Heat, stirring constantly. Add capers and asparagus spears; heat. Stir in sour cream until well blended. **Serve with Tiny dumplings, page 71 and boiled potatoes.**

Chicken à la Bohème

Böhmisches Huhn

3–4 servings

> 1 (2–3 lb.) roasting chicken
> ½ teaspoon salt
> 4 ounces vermicelli spaghetti,
>   cooked
> ¼ cup chopped parsley
> ¼ cup grated cheese
> 1 egg
> 1 tablespoon margarine or
>   butter
> 2 cups chicken bouillon

Wash and dry chicken; sprinkle salt in cavity. Mix cooked spaghetti, parsley, cheese, and egg; stuff chicken with mixture Rub margarine on chicken. Place in roasting pan on rack. Roast in (350°) oven for about 1½ hours or until chicken is done when tested. Remove chicken from pan. Cut in half lengthwise; place vermicelli stuffing on platter and place chicken halves on top. Pour bouillon into roasting pan and stir to combine with pan juices; serve as gravy.

Chicken poached with vegetables and herbs

Huhn mit Gemüse und Kräuter

8 servings

> 2 (2–3 lb.) frying chickens cut
>   into serving pieces
> 1 tablespoon flour
> 1 teaspoon salt
> ⅛ teaspoon pepper
> ¼ pound bacon, diced
> 1 medium onion, chopped
> 1 medium carrot, chopped
> ¼ cup chopped parsley
> 1 medium sized tart apple,
>   cored and chopped or
> ¼ cup canned apple slices,
>   chopped
> 6 peppercorns
> 1 bay leaf
> ½ teaspoon whole dried thyme
> ½ cup dry white wine
>   Hot cooked noodles

Sprinkle flour in cooking bag large enough to contain chicken pieces comfortably. Sprinkle chicken with salt and pepper. Cook diced bacon in large skillet until crisp. Add chopped vegetables and apple; cook over medium heat until transparent. Add peppercorns, bay leaf and thyme. Spread mixture in cooking bag in pan with 2" sides. Place chicken pieces on vegetables; add wine. Close bag with twist tie; puncture bag with sharp-tined fork 3 or 4 times. Place pan with bag in moderately slow oven (325°) until chicken is tender and slightly browned, about 1 hour. Serve with hot buttered noodles.

Chicken ragout

Bremer Kükenragout

8 servings

> 8 frying chicken parts (legs,
>   breasts or both)
> 1 teaspoon salt
> ¼ cup margarine or butter
> 2 cups chicken bouillon or
>   hot water
> 2 tablespoons flour
> 1 pound frozen, cooked,
>   shelled and deveined shrimp
> 1 (10 oz.) package frozen peas
>   with sliced mushrooms
> 1 (8½ oz.) can cut asparagus
>   pieces, drained
> ¼ cup sour cream
> 1 tablespoon lemon juice

Sprinkle chicken parts with salt. Melt margarine in frying pan; brown chicken pieces on all sides. Pour in bouillon, cover, and simmer over moderate heat about 15 minutes, until chicken is tender. Remove chicken to warm platter. Pour off bouillon and measure 1½ cups. (Any additional bouillon may be used for soups or in other recipes). In a saucepan, stir a small amount of the bouillon into the flour. Add remaining bouillon gradually. Cook over medium heat, stirring contantly, until thickened. Add frozen shrimp, cover and simmer until shrimp are thawed. Stir in peas and mushrooms, sour cream and asparagus. Heat gently, but do not allow to boil. Taste. If desired, add lemon juice. Serve hot over chicken pieces with mashed potatoes and a green salad.

Pomeranian roast goose

Pommerscher Gänsebraten

4–6 servings

> 1 (8–9 lb.) goose
> 1 onion, chopped
> 1 tablespoon salt
> 1½ cups pitted prunes, halved
> 4 tart apples, peeled, cored and quartered
> 1 cup coarse rye bread crumbs
> 2 tablespoons sugar
> 4 tablespoons flour

Wash and dry goose. Remove giblets; place in 1 quart saucepan with onion and 1 teaspoon salt. Cover with water. Simmer, partially covered, about 1–1½ hours. Strain; reserve stock. Sprinkle goose inside and out with salt. Combine prunes, apples, rye bread and sugar; fill cavity of bird. Skewer openings together. Place on rack in shallow roasting pan, breast side down. Roast in a hot oven (400°) 45 minutes. Drain fat from roasting pan. Reduce oven temperature to 325°; roast until tender when pierced with a fork, and juices are light yellow, not pink, about 1 hour. Drain fat from pan. Turn goose breast side up; brown until golden, about 30 minutes. Remove; keep warm. Skim off remaining fat. Stir flour into 2 cups stock; add to drippings in pan. Cook over medium heat, stirring and scraping browned bits, until thickened. Serve with goose.

There are always numbers of geese wobbling about the farmyards of the large old Pomeranian farms of East Germany. Goose tastes best if prepared in November or December, and it should always be cooked in its own fat.

The goose is the favorite German fowl. In the small villages and towns of the countryside they make a charming and amusing sight as they walk in long lines along the streets. Geese are anything but stupid, though they are often maligned. In ancient times, the loud warning given by a gaggle of alert geese is said to have prevented the treacherous overthrow of the Roman capitol. A Scottish whiskey distillery still uses geese to watch over their precious stocks because these sensitive birds seem to do the job far better than dogs. During the Middle Ages geese were trained to rotate the large roasting spits used for preparing wild pigs: the geese held one end of the spit in their beaks and turned it by thrusting their necks in and out. The idea that geese are stupid is obviously an injustice perpetuated by the ignorant.
A goose roasted in the German way, with apples, prunes and herbs, is a dish fit for a king and is one of the very favorite Christmas dinners in Germany.

Thuringian roast goose

Thüringer Gans

4–6 servings

> 1 (8–9 lb.) goose, fresh or frozen
> 1 tablespoon salt
> 1 teaspoon dried marjoram
> 2 medium onions, peeled
> 1 stalk celery, broken into 3–4 pieces
> Salt
> Pepper
> 6 cloves
> 2 apples, well washed
> 1 cup chicken or goose stock or water
> 1 cup orange juice
> 2 tablespoons cornstarch
> ¼ cup cold water

Thaw goose, if frozen. Remove giblets; place in 1-qt. saucepan with one of the onions, celery pieces, salt and pepper. Cover with water. Simmer, partially covered, for about 1–1½ hours. Strain; reserve stock. Meanwhile, wash and dry goose; sprinkle inside and out with salt. Sprinkle marjoram inside, stick cloves in second onion and place in cavity with the apples. Skewer openings together. Place goose on a rack in a large roasting pan, breast side down. Roast in a hot oven (400°) for 45 minutes. Drain fat from roasting pan. Reduce oven temperature to 325° and roast until tender when pierced with a fork and juices are light yellow, not pink, about 1 hour. Drain fat from pan. Turn goose breast side up on rack; brown in oven until golden, about 30 minutes. Remove to a warm platter. Skim off remaining fat. Add stock or water and orange juice to pan juices. Mix cornstarch and cold water, add to pan. Cook over medium heat, stirring constantly, until gravy is thickened.

Roast stuffed turkey

Festlicher Putenbraten

8–10 servings

1 tablespoon margarine or
  butter
1 large onion, chopped
1 apple, peeled, cored and
  chopped
1 pound ground pork
½ pound sausage meat
8 dried apricots, halved
8 prunes, pitted and halved
1 (8 oz.) package stuffing mix
1 cup apple juice or water
1 (10–12 lb.) turkey
1 onion, quartered
1 stalk celery, chopped
2 teaspoons salt
4 tablespoons flour

Melt margarine in large skillet;
sauté onion and apple in
margarine until onion is
transparent. Add meat; cook
until lightly browned, stirring
constantly. Add fruit, stuffing
mix and juice; blend lightly.
Remove giblets from turkey;
place in 1 quart saucepan with
onion, celery and 1 teaspoon
salt. Cover with water. Simmer,
covered, about 1–1½ hours.
Strain; reserve stock. Rub neck
and body cavities of turkey
lightly with remaining teaspoon
salt. Stuff neck and body
cavities lightly with stuffing;

skewer openings shut. Place
turkey, breast side up, on rack
in shallow roasting pan. Insert
meat thermometer in thigh
muscle. Place a loose tent of
foil over bird (remove last 30
minutes). Roast in a slow oven
(325°) about 2½–3 hours or
until thermometer reads 185°.
Move drumstick up and down;
if it moves easily, bird is done.
Place bird on warm platter.
Drain off fat. Stir flour into
2 cups stock; add to drippings.
Cook over medium heat,
stirring constantly, until
thickened.

Roast duckling with apples

Vierländer Mastente

4–6 servings

1 (4–5 lb.) frozen duckling
  thawed
1 teaspoon salt
¼ teaspoon black pepper
4 apples, thinly sliced and
  peeled
2–3 slices day-old bread, cubed
½ teaspoon poultry seasoning
¼ cup blackberry brandy
  (or orange juice)
1 onion, sliced

Thoroughly wash duck.
Sprinkle inside cavity with salt
and pepper. Mix apple slices,
bread cubes, poultry seasoning
and brandy. Stuff duck with
mixture. Place on rack in
roasting pan. Prick breast with
fork. Place onion in pan around
duck. Roast, uncovered, at
(325°) for 2½–3 hours. Pour off
fat as it accumulates. Baste
occasionally with pan drippings.
Serve with baked stuffed
apples, if desired.

Roast duckling with apples

Berlin style duckling

Ente, Berliner Art

4 servings

1 frozen duckling (about 5
  pounds), thawed
1½ teaspoons salt
¼ teaspoon black pepper
½ teaspoon powdered marjoram
4 tart apples, peeled, cored
  and quartered
¾ cup hot water
1 tablespoon cornstarch
2 tablespoons cold water

Wash and dry thawed duckling.
Sprinkle inside and out with
salt and pepper. Sprinkle
marjoram inside, place apples
in cavity and skewer shut.
Pour water into roasting pan.
Place duckling breast side down
in pan. Roast in moderate oven
(350°) for about 40 minutes.
Pour off fat. Baste frequently
with pan juices. Turn duck over,
cook another 50–60 minutes or
until thigh is tender when
pierced with a fork and juices
are yellow, not pink. Remove
duck to a warm platter. Pour
off fat. Measure drippings,
make up to 1 cup with water
or stock. Stir cornstarch into
cold water, add to pan juices.
Cook over medium heat,
stirring constantly, until
thickened. Serve with carved
duckling.

Giblet and pork stew

Braunschweiger Geflügelklein

4 servings

3 cloves
1 medium onion, peeled
1½ pounds chicken giblets
  (hearts, livers, gizzards,
  necks and wings)
1 quart water
½ teaspoon salt
1 small bay leaf
½ pound sausage meat
¼ cup margarine or butter
3 tablespoons flour
1 cup milk
1 teaspoon grated lemon rind
1 (8½ oz.) can cut asparagus
  pieces, drained
1 (6 oz.) can sliced
  mushrooms, drained

Stick cloves into onion. Wash
and trim giblets. Place onion,
giblets, water, salt and bay leaf
into a saucepan. Simmer,
uncovered, until giblets are
tender, about 1 hour. Drain,
reserving 1 cup liquid. Cut
giblets and pieces of chicken
meat into 1″ pieces. Shape
sausage meat into 1″ balls.
In frying pan, over medium
heat, brown sausage balls on
all sides. Melt margarine in
saucepan. Stir in flour, gradually
add the 1 cup reserved liquid
and milk, stirring constantly,
until sauce is thickened, about
2–3 minutes. Stir in lemon
rind, giblets, sausage balls,
asparagus and mushrooms.
Cook over low heat until hot.
Do not boil. Serve with
rice and peas.

Roast Rock-Cornish hens

Gebratene Hähnchen

4 servings

4 (1–lb.) frozen Rock-Cornish
  hens, thawed
1 teaspoon salt
¼ teaspoon black pepper
4 slices bacon, diced
2 slices day-old bread
⅓ cup milk
1 tablespoon chopped parsley
5 tablespoons margarine or
  butter
1 cup beef bouillon
1 tablespoon flour
½ cup sour cream

Wash and dry hens. Rub inside
cavities with salt and pepper.
In a skillet, cook bacon until
crisp. Brown the livers of the
hens; chop into small pieces.
Soften bread in milk and
squeeze out. Add bacon,
chopped livers, and parsley.
Stuff hens with mixture. Melt
margarine in roasting pan
and brown each hen. Roast in
moderate oven (350°) for 1–1½
hours or until hens are
cooked. Remove hens and keep
warm. Pour bouillon into
roasting pan and stir over direct
heat to loosen drippings. Stir
in flour. Cook until slightly
thickened. Stir in sour cream.
Serve gravy with roast hens.

Rock-Cornish hens, Berlin style

Hähnchen Berliner Art

4 servings

4 (1¼ lb.) frozen Rock-
  Cornish hens, thawed
1 (6 oz.) package rice and
  wild rice, prepared
  according to package
  directions
1 small onion, chopped
1 stalk celery, finely chopped
½ cup seedless grapes, halved
½ cup slivered almonds
½ teaspoon salt
½ teaspoon thyme
¼ cup melted margarine or
  butter

Wash and dry hens. Combine
rice, onion, celery, grapes,
almonds, salt and thyme; mix
well. Fill neck and body
cavities lightly with stuffing;
skewer openings shut. Place
hens in large shallow roasting
pan; brush with melted
margarine. Roast hens in a hot
oven (400°) about 1 hour or
until well browned and
drumstick twists easily out of
thigh joint, basting several
times with margarine.

*To really enjoy a game dinner in
the authentic fashion, one must go
to one of the many old castles.
There are still hundreds of them
spread all over Germany: old
knight's castles and elegant small
hunter's castles from the
Eighteenth Century. In recent
years, the upkeep of these places
has become so expensive that
many of them have been converted
into hotels or restaurants by their
owners, whose families and
ancestors may have lived there for
centuries. In the knights' hall of
the castle, a romantic evening is
relived just as it took place in the
distant past.*

*The flames dance in the fireplace
and the whole hall gives off the
aroma of wild game. The table is
beautifully decked and wine from
the surrounding vineyards*

Pheasant, Baden style

Fasan, Badische Art

4 servings

1 (2¼–3 lb.) pheasant
1½ teaspoons salt
¼ cup melted margarine or
  butter
1 tablespoon brandy
1 teaspoon grated lemon rind
¼ teaspoon powdered thyme
1½ cups water
1 tablespoon flour

Wash pheasant; dry well.
Sprinkle ½ teaspoon salt over
insides of bird. Place bird on
rack in shallow roasting pan.
Combine margarine, brandy,
rind, ½ teaspoon salt and
thyme; brush bird generously.
Roast in a moderately hot oven
(375°) about 55 minutes,
basting bird frequently with
margarine mixture. Combine
giblets, water and remaining
salt in saucepan; cook until
tender. Remove giblets. Strain
broth; save. Remove bird;
skim off fat. Stir flour into 1
cup broth; return to pan.
Cook over low heat, stirring
constantly, until thickened.
Serve with pheasant.

*sparkles in large goblets. In the
small hunters' castles, the guests
eat in elegant, cozy dining halls,
accompanying their food with
plentiful quantities of wine. From
gold-framed portraits hanging
over the fireplace, ancestral faces
in powdered wigs stare down
stonily on the strangers sitting
around their tables, where
fragrant lilies of the valley stand
amidst the family silverware and
crystal. Everything served is
'hausgemacht'—homemade—from
the inviting berry jam at breakfast
and the ham and trout at dinner to
the tart at dessert and the plum
brandy served with the evening
coffee.*

Rabbit paté en croûte

Schwäbische Kaninchenpastete

8 servings

*   *1 (2–2½ lb.) package frozen rabbit, thawed and boned*
*   *4 tablespoons margarine or butter*
*   *1 onion, peeled and cut into 6 wedges*
*   *1 clove garlic, crushed (if desired)*
*   *½ cup chopped parsley*
*   *1 (6 oz.) can sliced mushrooms, drained*
*   *¼ teaspoon thyme*
*   *½ cup dry white wine*
*   *1 (10 oz.) package frozen puff-paste patty shells*
*   *1 egg, beaten lightly*

Heat margarine in skillet. Over medium heat, brown rabbit meat on all sides. Put meat and onion through food grinder, using fine blade. Combine with garlic, parsley, mushrooms, thyme, wine and the margarine remaining in skillet. Blend well. Roll out the thawed patty shells to ⅛″ thick. Carefully line a 9″ × 5″ × 3″ loaf pan with the pastry; moisten edges slightly and press together firmly. Fill the pastry-lined pan with the rabbit mixture. Fold pastry over top and seal tightly. With point of knife, make three ½″ holes in top for steam vents. Brush beaten egg over surface. Bake in moderate oven (350°) about 1 hour. Cool and turn out of pan. Serve warm or cool.

Silesian roast hare

Schlesischer Hasenbraten

4–6 servings

*   *1 (2½–3 lb.) package frozen rabbit parts, thawed*
*   *4 slices bacon, diced*
*   *1 teaspoon salt*
*   *¼ teaspoon black pepper*
*   *¼ teaspoon nutmeg*
*   *¼ teaspoon thyme*
*   *¼ cup flour*
*   *2 slices pimiento, diced*
*   *1 cup water*
*   *½ cup sour cream*

Wash and dry pieces of rabbit. Brown diced bacon; drain on paper towels. Reserve bacon drippings. Place salt, pepper, nutmeg, thyme, and flour in a paper bag. Shake rabbit parts in bag until fully coated with seasoned flour. Brown in bacon drippings. Add pimiento and cook until all parts are tender. Remove rabbit and keep warm. Pour water into pan and heat, scraping pan to blend. Stir in sour cream. Add crisp pieces of bacon. Serve rabbit with hot gravy.

Rabbit in wine gravy

Hasenpfeffer

4 servings

*   *1 (2½–3 lb.) rabbit, cut up*
*   *2 cups red wine*
*   *1 cup water*
*   *¼ cup vinegar*
*   *1 onion, sliced*
*   *1 tablespoon sugar*
*   *2 tablespoons salt*
*   *1 teaspoon whole cloves*
*   *¼ teaspoon black pepper*
*   *3 bay leaves*
*   *½ cup flour*
*   *¼ cup salad oil*

Place rabbit in large bowl.

Combine wine, water, vinegar, onion, sugar, salt, cloves, pepper and bay leaves; pour over meat. Place in refrigerator; marinate 12–24 hours. Remove rabbit; dry well. Dredge rabbit with flour; save remaining flour. Heat oil in Dutch oven. Brown rabbit in hot oil. Strain marinade; add 2½ cups to rabbit. Cover; simmer 1 hour or until meat is tender. Remove rabbit; keep warm. If a thicker sauce is desired, stir in remaining flour. Cook over medium heat, stirring constantly, until sauce is thickened. Serve over meat.

Mixed meat and vegetable stew

Mixed meat and vegetable stew

Pichelsteiner Topf

6 servings

    4 slices bacon, diced
    4 carrots, peeled and quartered
    2 large onions, sliced
    ½ pound beef, cut into 1" cubes
    ½ pound lamb, cut into 1" cubes
    ½ pound pork, cut into 1" cubes
    3 large potatoes, peeled and
       cubed
    4 cups beef bouillon
    ½ teaspoon salt
    ¼ teaspoon black pepper
    ¼ teaspoon dried marjoram
    2 tablespoons chopped parsley

Cook bacon in large Dutch oven
until crisp; drain off fat. Place
alternate layers of carrots,
onions, meat and potatoes in
Dutch oven. Add bouillon, salt,
pepper and marjoram. Bring
to a boil; cover; reduce heat
and simmer about 1½ hours.
Garnish with parsley before
serving.

Corned beef hash with eggs

Labskaus

4 servings

    2 (15½ oz.) cans corned beef
       hash
    ½ cup chopped dill pickle
    ½ cup chopped pickled herring
    2 tablespoons margarine or
       butter
    4 fried or poached eggs

Combine hash, pickles, and
herring; mix lightly. Melt
margarine in large skillet.
Spoon hash mixture into
skillet; spread evenly in pan.
Cook over low heat, stirring
occasionally until hash is well
browned. Top each serving of
hash with a cooked egg.

Heaven and earth

Himmel und Erde

4–6 servings

    1 teaspoon grated lemon rind
    2½ cups (28 oz. jar) applesauce
    2 cups mashed hot potatoes
    ¼ pound bacon, diced
    2 large onions, sliced
    ½ teaspoon salt
    ⅛ teaspoon black pepper
       Blood sausage slices, or
       liver slices, cooked

Stir lemon rind into applesauce.
Mix with hot potatoes. Keep
hot. Fry bacon in large skillet.
Add sliced onions, cook over
medium heat until transparent
and golden brown. Stir into hot
potato mixture. Add salt and
pepper. Serve hot with hot
blood sausage slices or liver.

Shoemaker's pot

Köthener Schusterpfanne

4 servings

    2 pounds boneless pork loin
       roast
    1 teaspoon salt
    ⅛ teaspoon pepper
    3 large potatoes, peeled and
       cut into 1" cubes
    3 large green ripe pears,
       peeled and cut into eighths
       or 12 small ripe Seckel
       pears, peeled, cored, and
       halved
    ¼ teaspoon dried marjoram
    ¼ teaspoon dried dill weed
    1 tablespoon caraway seed
    1 tablespoon thick liquid beef
       broth and seasoning base
    2 cups boiling water
    2 tablespoons cornstarch
    ¼ cup cold water

Sprinkle pork with salt and
pepper; place in Dutch oven.
Arrange potatoes and pears
around meat. Sprinkle marjoram,
dill and caraway seed over all.
Dissolve seasoning base in
boiling water; pour into Dutch
oven; cover tightly. Bring to a
boil; reduce heat; simmer
about 1½ hours or until meat is
tender when pierced with a
fork. Remove meat, potatoes
and pears to a warm platter.
Stir cornstarch into cold water.
Add to liquid in Dutch oven.
Cook over medium heat,
stirring constantly, until sauce
is thickened. Serve over meat.

*'Labskaus' (corned beef hash) is
an ancient sailor's dish which
originated on the vessels coasting
along the north coast of Germany
and Scandinavia.*

Corned beef hash with egg

Cabbage and bacon casserole

Rothenburger Krautbraten

4–6 servings

1 medium head white cabbage, core removed
1 bay leaf
9 slices bacon
1½ pounds potatoes, **sliced**
1 pound ground beef
½ cup coarse white bread crumbs
1 teaspoon salt
⅛ teaspoon pepper
½ teaspoon paprika
1 teaspoon caraway seed
½ cup half-and-half
2 egg yolks
2 tablespoons flour
½ teaspoon salt
Dash black pepper

Cook whole cabbage in boiling salted water to which bay leaf has been added, about 5 minutes, or until outside cabbage leaves are tender. Drain well; carefully remove 5 or 6 outside cabbage leaves. Cut remaining cabbage into thin strips. Line a 5-quart casserole with bacon slices. Arrange cabbage leaves over bacon. Spread half the potatoes over cabbage leaves. Mix together beef, bread crumbs, salt, pepper, paprika and caraway seed. Alternate layers of meat mixture and finely cut cabbage. Cover with remaining potatoes. Beat together cream, egg yolks, flour, salt and pepper; pour over potatoes. Cover tightly. Bake in a moderate oven (350°) 45–60 minutes, or until potatoes are tender. Serve hot.

Sauerkraut and frankfurter casserole

Sauerkraut-Auflauf

6 servings

2 tablespoons salad oil
1 cup sliced onion, about 2 medium
1 (1 lb.) can sauerkraut
¼ cup beef bouillon or water
¼ pound sausage meat
¼ cup dehydrated potato flakes
⅓ cup Liebfraumilch wine
½ teaspoon sugar
3 slices bacon, cut into 1" pieces
2 small tart apples, cored, peeled and cut into ½" rings
2 cups mashed potatoes
¼ pound (2–2½) frankfurters, sliced into ½" pieces
2 tablespoons margarine or butter

Heat oil in large skillet. Sauté onions in hot fat over medium heat, until transparent. Add sauerkraut and bouillon. Cover; simmer about 25–30 minutes or until liquid has almost completely evaporated. Break up sausage meat into small pieces; stir into sauerkraut mixture; blend in potato flakes, then wine and sugar. Bring to a boil; simmer 1 minute; set aside. Fry bacon until browned. Remove bacon pieces; drain on paper towels. Add apple rings; sauté until browned and tender, about 2–3 minutes. Spread 1 cup mashed potatoes in bottom of greased 2-quart casserole. Cover with half the sauerkraut mixture; then the apples and bacon pieces. Spread remaining sauerkraut over these. Top with remaining mashed potatoes. Dot with margarine. Bake in a moderate oven (350°) 45 minutes or until potatoes are lightly browned.

Hunters' casserole

Bayerischer Jägertopf

4 servings

1½ pounds beef for stew
½ teaspoon salt
⅛ teaspoon black pepper
2 large onions, chopped
1 (6 oz.) can sliced mushrooms, drained
½ cup dry red wine
1 cup beef bouillon
3 carrots, sliced
3 medium potatoes, sliced

Sprinkle meat with salt and pepper. Heat oil in heavy saucepot. Brown meat well in hot oil. Add onions and mushrooms; cook until onions are transparent. Add wine; cover; simmer 30 minutes. Add bouillon; continue to simmer 30 minutes. Add carrots and potatoes; stir well. Cook, covered, 20–25 minutes or until vegetables are tender.

Cabbage and bacon casserole

Frankfurt noodle casserole

Frankfurter Nudelpfanne

6 servings

1 (8 oz.) package noodles,
  cooked and drained
1 (10 oz.) package frozen
  peas, thawed
4 tablespoons margarine or
  butter
1 (10 oz.) package frozen
  spinach, cooked and drained
1 pound frankfurters, sliced
1 (10½ oz.) can cream of
  mushroom soup
½ cup sour cream
½ cup milk
4 slices bacon, cooked and
  crumbled

Combine noodles, 1½ cups peas,
and margarine; mix lightly.
Place spinach in bottom of
buttered 2½ qt. casserole.
Spread noodle mixture over
spinach. Combine frankfurters,
soup, sour cream, and milk;
mix well; pour over noodles.
Bake in a hot oven (400°) about
25 minutes. Sprinkle bacon and
peas over top; bake 5 minutes
more.

*Frankfurt noodle casserole.
When Germans invite friends out
for cocktails, they always serve
a warm casserole just before the
guests leave. It gives them the
courage to face the long trip
home.*

Vegetable Dishes & Dumplings

Vegetable medley

Vegetable medley

Spinach filled pancakes

Leipziger Allerlei

8 servings

- 2 cups beef bouillon
- 1 (10 oz.) package frozen cauliflower, separated
- 1 (10 oz.) package frozen peas
- 1 (10 oz.) package frozen asparagus, cut in half
- 1 (14 oz.) can baby carrots, drained
- 1 (3 oz.) can sliced mushrooms
- 4 tablespoons flour
- 2 teaspoons salt
- ¼ cup cold water
- 2 hard cooked eggs, peeled and quartered

Heat bouillon in large saucepan. Add vegetables; simmer 8–10 minutes. Add flour and salt to water; blend until smooth; stir into vegetables. Cook over low heat, stirring constantly, until thickened. Pour into serving dish. Garnish with eggs.

Nature often cooperates with cookery by arranging it so that different things which go well together grow next to each other. A nice instance of this occurs on the left bank of the Rhine between Worms and Nierstein. Here, in this wide valley, the thickest, whitest and most tender asparagus imaginable grow right alongside the grapevines that yield the soft, blond luxurious wines from Rheinhessen. Liebfraumilch is the most famous of these wines. Asparagus and wine make up one of the gourmet's favorite combinations.

The small hotels and inns in Oppenheim and Worms serve asparagus accompanied by a sparkling white wine in wide glasses on brown stems. To eat this superb asparagus in the grand manner, you can go aboard a Rheindampfer, one of the large white boats which make day trips up and down the Rhine. Here, from the large windows of the ship's dining room, you can regard the slowly moving landscape of green hills and old castles and enjoy the tender asparagus while the sun sparkles in your glass.

Pfälzer Pfannkuchen-Auflauf

4 servings

- 1 cup biscuit-type baking mix
- 1 egg
- ¾ cup milk
- 1 (10 oz.) package frozen spinach, cooked and drained
- 2 tablespoons margarine or butter
- ⅛ teaspoon salt
- ⅛ teaspoon black pepper
  Dash nutmeg
- ½ cup evaporated milk
- 1 cup (4 oz.) shredded Swiss cheese

Combine baking mix, egg and milk; beat until smooth. Drop by ⅓ cup measures onto hot griddle. Cook over low heat until rim is full of broken bubbles; turn; brown on other side. Remove; keep warm. Combine spinach, margarine, salt, pepper and nutmeg; mix well. Spread spinach mixture on pancakes; roll. Place in greased 11¾″ × 7½″ × 1¾″ baking dish. Heat evaporated milk; add cheese. Cook, stirring constantly, until cheese is melted; pour over pancakes. Bake in a hot oven (400°) about 8–10 minutes or until lightly browned.

Spinach filled pancakes

Potato cake

Lappenpickert

6–8 servings

4 cups firmly packed, peeled,
  grated and drained
  potatoes (about 2 lbs.)
2 eggs, slightly beaten
3 tablespoons flour
1 teaspoon salt
⅓ cup sour cream
¼ cup salad oil

Put grated potatoes into mixing
bowl. Add eggs, flour, salt and
sour cream. Beat with mixing
spoon until well blended.
Heat 2 tablespoons of the oil
in each of 2 large skillets until
very hot. Carefully spread half
the potato mixture in each
skillet, about ½″ thick. Cook
over moderately high heat until
browned on bottom. Carefully
turn over. (If necessary, cut
into quarters and turn each
quarter separately.) Add more
oil, if needed. Cook until
browned. Serve immediately.
If desired, wrap cooled potato
sections in waxed paper. May
be reheated in a little oil over
moderate heat. Serve either as a
meat accompaniment or with
jelly or syrup.

Lentils and bacon

Berliner Linsentopf

8 servings

2¼ cups (1 lb.) lentils, washed
  and cleaned
6 cups water
1 pound thick sliced bacon,
  cut into 1″ pieces
3 medium-sized potatoes (1
  pound) peeled, cut into
  ½″ cubes
½ cup vinegar
¼ cup sugar
  Salt, if needed
2 tablespoons margarine or
  butter
2 medium onions, finely
  chopped
2 tablespoons chopped parsley

Combine lentils, water and
bacon in large heavy saucepan.
Bring to a boil; reduce heat.
Cover; simmer 45 minutes.
Add potatoes, continue to cook
until lentils and potatoes are
tender, about 15 minutes.
Stir in vinegar and sugar.
Taste, add salt, if needed.
Place in serving dish; keep
hot. Melt margarine in skillet;
sauté onions and parsley over
medium heat until onions are
transparent, 2–3 minutes.
Spoon over lentils. Serve hot.

Westphalian white cabbage

Westfälischer Weißkohl

4–6 servings

4 tablespoons margarine or
  butter
4 medium onions, chopped
1 small head cabbage, chopped
2 green apples, peeled and
  chopped
1 tablespoon vinegar
1 teaspoon sugar
1 teaspoon salt
¼ teaspoon black pepper
2¾ cups hot water
¼ cup instant mashed potato

Melt margarine in skillet; add
onion and cook until golden
brown. In a large saucepan,
make alternate layers of cabbage
and apple. Add vinegar, sugar,
salt and pepper. Pour 2 cups
of the hot water over cabbage
mixture. Cover tightly, bring
to a boil, and simmer for 30
minutes. Add instant potatoes
to remaining ¾ cup hot water.
Stir potatoes and onion into
hot cabbage. Serve warm.

Westphalian white cabbage

70

Bavarian potato dumplings

Bayerische Kartoffelknödel

6–8 servings

    2 pounds potatoes, peeled
      and boiled
    ⅓ cup margarine or butter
    ⅛ teaspoon salt
    1 egg yolk
    ¾ to 1 cup sifted flour
    1 slice white bread, cut into
      1" cubes
    1 tablespoon margarine or
      butter

Mash potatoes until very smooth with margarine and salt. Beat in egg and flour adding enough flour to make an easily handled dough. Fry cubes of bread in 1 tablespoon margarine, browning both sides. Form approximately 2" balls of the potato dough. Press a cube of fried bread into center of each potato ball and smooth surface. Bring a large kettle of water to a boil. Drop potato balls carefully into boiling water. Bring water back to a boil, lower heat and simmer for 20 minutes. Dumplings should float and be slightly puffed up when done. Drain on paper towels. Serve immediately with sauerbraten or pot roast and gravy, recipes page 49.

On any fine Sunday near the end of the summer or the beginning of fall, you can see German children roaming through the woods with baskets under their arms. They collect mushrooms, especially the beautiful, orange-yellow 'Pfifferlinge' which are always eaten with bread dumplings.

Bread dumplings with mushrooms

Semmelknödel mit Pilzen

4–6 servings

    1 recipe bread dumplings,
      see following recipe
    ¼ cup margarine or butter
    1 pound fresh mushrooms,
      sliced
    ½ cup chopped parsley
    2 tablespoons flour
    1 cup half-and-half
    ½ teaspoon salt
      Dash black pepper

Prepare dumplings according to **following recipe**. Meanwhile, melt margarine in large skillet. Sauté mushrooms in margarine until tender, about 10 minutes. Add parsley. Sprinkle flour over mushrooms. Gradually stir in half-and-half. Cook over medium heat, stirring constantly, until thickened. Season with salt and pepper. Serve over dumplings.

Bavarian bread dumplings

Bayerische Semmelknödel

Makes 18

    1 (14 oz.) loaf day-old
      French bread
    1 cup milk
    2 eggs, beaten
    1 teaspoon salt
    ⅓ cup finely chopped onions
    1 tablespoon parsley
    3 quarts salted water

Cut bread into very thin slices; soak in milk. Add eggs and salt; let stand 30 minutes. Add onion and parsley. Blend to an even consistency. In a large, wide saucepan, bring salted water to a boil; reduce to a simmer. Shape dumplings with wet hands to about the size of a small egg. (If mixture is too soft, add some dry bread crumbs to it.) Drop dumplings into simmering water, being careful not to crowd dumplings. Cover and simmer for 10–15 minutes. Keep warm. Serve with meat and gravy.

Liver dumplings

Leberknödel

4–6 servings

    ½ pound baby beef liver,
      trimmed
    2 cups packaged stuffing mix
    1 cup warm water
    ¼ pound bacon, diced
    1 large onion, chopped
    2 eggs
    1 teaspoon salt
      Salted water or bouillon

Put liver through meat grinder. Soften stuffing mix in warm water. Fry bacon; add onion; cook over medium heat until onion is transparent. Mix together liver, softened stuffing, cooked bacon and onion, eggs and salt. (Add a little crushed dry stuffing mix if not quite firm enough to hold its shape.) Drop by ½ teaspoonfuls into gently boiling salted water or bouillon. Cook until tender, about 10 minutes. (Dumplings will rise to surface of water when done.) Serve with melted margarine or butter, if desired.

Bread dumplings with mushrooms

Tiny dumplings

Schwäbische Spätzle

4–6 servings

 2 *eggs, slightly beaten*
 1 *cup water*
 1 *teaspoon salt*
 3 *cups flour*

Combine eggs, water, salt, and flour. Beat until dough is thick and smooth. Add more flour if necessary. In a large saucepan, bring 2–3 quarts of salted water to a boil. Place ⅓ of the dough on a small, wet chopping board. With a sharp knife, cut thin strips (¾″ × 2½″) one at a time, slipping off board directly into boiling water. Repeat until all dough is used. Do not crowd in boiling water. Dumplings are done when they float. Remove from boiling water; rinse with hot water and keep warm. Serve with meat and gravy.

Rhenish potato pancakes

Rheinische Puffer

3 dozen 3″ pancakes

 2 *pounds large potatoes, peeled and cut into 2″ pieces*
 1 *medium onion, cut into 6 wedges*
 2 *eggs*
 1 *teaspoon salt*
  Cooking oil

Break eggs into blender jar; start blending at high speed. Partially covering top, add one piece of potato at a time, 1–2 seconds apart, adding a piece of onion frequently. Add salt. Blend one minute. Heat a thin film of oil in griddle or skillet over moderately high heat. Add more oil as needed. For each pancake, spread a heaping tablespoon potato mixture into a 3″ circle; brown on both sides. Drain on paper towels. Keep warm until all are completed. Serve immediately.

Buttered asparagus

Stangenspargel

4 servings

 2 *pounds white asparagus*
 1½ *teaspoons salt*
 1 *teaspoon sugar*
 ¼ *cup melted margarine or butter*
 1 *hard cooked egg, finely chopped, optional*

Arrange asparagus in 2 layers in 9″ or 10″ skillet. Sprinkle with salt and sugar. Pour on 1″ boiling water. Boil, uncovered, 5 minutes; cover and cook 7–10 minutes longer, or until just tender crisp when tested with a fork. Carefully lift out asparagus; arrange on serving dish. Pour melted margarine over asparagus. Garnish with chopped egg if desired.

Braised sauerkraut

Sauerkraut

4 servings

 ¼ *cup margarine or butter*
 1 *medium onion, chopped*
 3 *cups sauerkraut, drained*
 2 *cups beef bouillon*
 2 *apples, sliced*
 2 *slices bacon*
 1 *potato, grated*

Melt margarine in large skillet. Sauté onion until golden brown. Stir in sauerkraut and apple slices. Pour in bouillon and place bacon slices on top. Cover; simmer for 30–40 minutes. Add grated potato and continue to simmer until mixture thickens, stirring constantly. Remove bacon and serve hot.

Buttered asparagus

Sauerkraut is a very versatile dish in Germany; it is served in winter and summer, in the humblest kitchens and the best restaurants, with ham, bacon, partridge, goose and with different kinds of sausages. Hot sauerkraut with frankfurters is the traditional snack eaten in train stations and wayside restaurants along the turnpikes and highways.

Braised cucumbers

Hannoversches Gurkengemüse

4 servings

¼ cup margarine or butter
1 tablespoon sugar
½ teaspoon salt
2 large cucumbers, peeled and
 cut into 2″ pieces
1 medium onion, chopped
2 tomatoes, quartered
¼ cup water
1 teaspoon lemon juice
¼ teaspoon dill weed
½ cup sour cream

Melt margarine in large
saucepan. Add sugar and salt;
cook until lightly browned.
Add cucumbers and onion.
Cook, stirring constantly, until
onions are transparent. Add
tomatoes, water, lemon juice,
and dill weed. Cook 10–12
minutes. Stir in sour cream.
Serve immediately.

*Because we almost always eat
cucumber raw, we sometimes
forget that it makes an excellent
dish when braised.*

A good strudel is the pride of any Bavarian housewife. She probably stood around in the kitchen and learned the art from her mother when she was a small child.

Bavarian apple strudel

Bayerischer Apfelstrudel

18 servings

- 1 tablespoon oil
- 1 egg
- ⅓ cup warm water
- ¼ teaspoon salt
- 1½ cups sifted flour
- ⅓ cup melted margarine or butter
- 6 tablespoons fine dry bread crumbs
- 8 cups thinly sliced, peeled and cored tart apples
- 2 tablespoons dark rum
- 3 tablespoons sugar
- ½ teaspoon cinnamon
- ¼ cup finely chopped almonds
- ¼ cup seedless raisins
  Confectioners' sugar or whipped cream, optional

Beat together oil, egg, water and salt; add flour while beating, until a firm dough which pulls away from bowl is formed. Knead several times until smooth and elastic. Cover; let stand 30 minutes. Cut with sharp knife into two equal parts. Roll out each piece on floured cloth to a 12″ × 18″ rectangle. Brush with melted margarine. Sprinkle evenly with bread crumbs. Spread 4 cups of the apples on each portion, lengthwise down the center of the dough. Sprinkle each with 1 tablespoon rum, 1½ tablespoons sugar, ¼ teaspoon cinnamon, 2 tablespoons almonds and 2 tablespoons raisins. Fold dough over apples on one side, then the other. Slide rolls onto greased baking sheet. Brush with melted margarine. Bake in a hot oven (400°) 45 minutes. Cut each roll into 2″ slices. Serve warm or cold sprinkled with confectioners' sugar or with whipped cream, if desired.

Swabian apple cake

Schwäbischer Apfelkuchen

9″ cake

- 2 cups flour
- 1 cup sugar
- ½ teaspoon salt
- 1 cup margarine or butter
- 1 egg, slightly beaten
- 4 medium apples, sliced
- 1 tablespoon lemon juice
- 1 teaspoon lemon rind
- ⅓ cup raisins
- ½ cup almonds, chopped

Mix flour, ¼ cup of the sugar, and salt. Cut in ¾ cup of the margarine until size of grains of cornmeal. Stir in egg until dough forms a ball. Gather together with fingers, if necessary; knead together to form a smooth dough. Chill. Role ⅔ of dough out on lightly floured board to make an 11″ round. Fit into a 9″ round cake pan. Combine apple slices, lemon juice and rind, raisins, and ½ of the almonds. Fill pastry-lined pan with mixture. Roll remaining pastry into 9″ round. Place on top of apples. Pinch edges together. Heat remaining margarine, sugar, and almonds together in a small saucepan slowly until margarine melts and sugar dissolves. Spoon over top crust of cake. Place in moderate oven (350°) and bake for 45–50 minutes or until crust is golden brown.

Apple custard cake

Apfelkuchen mit Guß

One 8″ square cake

- ½ cup margarine or butter
- ¼ cup sugar
- 1 teaspoon cinnamon
- 1 cup sifted flour
- 1 egg
- 1 (3 oz.) package vanilla pudding mix
- 1½ cups milk
- 1 (22 oz.) can apple pie filling
- 1 tablespoon lemon juice
- ½ teaspoon grated lemon rind

Beat margarine and sugar well; add cinnamon and blend in flour. Divide dough in half. Press one half into buttered 8″ square baking pan. Add egg to other half; mix well. Prepare vanilla pudding according to package directions, using 1½ cups milk. Pour half over dough in pan. Stir lemon juice and rind into apple pie filling. Spread over vanilla pudding. Cover apples with remaining vanilla pudding. Sprinkle reserved crumbly egg-flour mixture evenly over pudding. Bake in a moderate oven (350°) for 35 minutes, or until top is lightly browned. Cool. Cut in squares. Serve warm or cool.

Baden apple roll

Badische Apfelrolle

8 servings

- 1 (10 oz.) package frozen puff pastry tarts, thawed
- ½ cup orange marmalade
- 3 medium apples, peeled and sliced
- 2 tablespoons chopped almonds
- 2 tablespoons raisins
- 2 tablespoons sugar
- 1 teaspoon cinnamon

Press dough together; roll out in a large rectangle about 12″ × 8″. Spread marmalade on surface of dough, leaving a 1″ margin on all sides. Place apples on top of marmalade on half of the dough. Sprinkle chopped almonds, raisins, sugar, and cinnamon on the apple slices. Fold other half of pastry over apples. Bake in a hot oven (400°) for 30–35 minutes or until pastry is lightly browned.

Germany has long been known for its many different kinds of pastry, but the most traditional are the 'Lebkuchen', golden-brown cakes, sweetened with honey and flavored with anise and other spices. They are sold at fairs and carnivals and at the Christmas markets.

These delicacies are baked in an endless array of shapes and forms, and many German museums have preserved cookie-boards of complex design that have been used to bake Lebkuchen for centuries. There are horses and carriages, hunters with their catch on their back, Saint Nicholas and the Christ Child, baskets of flowers, castles, Biblical scenes such as Adam and Eve in the garden of Eden, and the martyrdom of the Innocents at Bethlehem, and also lighter themes depicting Susan bathing, or a couple tenderly embracing each other.

Alas, this rich fantasy has given way to standard depictions of Saint Nicholas and of hearts decorated with red and white sugar rings or roses.

A Carnival would still be incomplete without Lebkuchen, and they also play an important role in weddings and village feasts. Sometimes small mirrors or red ribbons are baked into the cakes.

The most delicious Lebkuchen come from Nurnberg, which was an important junction for the spice merchants in the Middle Ages. The fortunate local bakers could therefore lay their hands on cinnamon and nutmeg, cloves and ginger, anise and cardamon – everything needed to prepare the most delicious Lebkuchen.

See recipe for christmas spice cookies, page 75.

Christmas spice cookies

Nürnberger Lebkuchen

2 dozen 2″ cookies

2 eggs
1 cup sugar
1 cup sifted flour
¼ teaspoon cinnamon
⅛ teaspoon ground cloves
⅛ teaspoon powdered
  cardamom
¾ cup blanched almonds,
  chopped fine in blender
¼ cup candied lemon peel
½ teaspoon grated lemon peel

Beat eggs, gradually add sugar
and beat until thickened.
Blend in flour, spices, almonds
and lemon peels. Drop by
teaspoonful on well greased
cookie sheets, or spread in
a well greased 8″ square baking
pan. Bake in a slow oven (325°)
15–20 minutes or until edges are
beginning to brown for drop
cookies; 20–25 minutes or until
edges begin to pull away from
sides of pan for bar cookies.
Remove from cookie sheet; cool
on rack. Or, cut into bars about
3″ × 1″ (make 3 cuts in one
direction, 8 in the other).
Cool on rack. Store cookies
or bars in cookie jar to mellow
for a few days. Cookies may
be sprinkled with powdered
sugar or iced with a chocolate
glaze.

Almond paste cookies

Almond paste cookies

Königsberger Marzipan

Makes 30 2″ cookies

Cookies:
3 cups finely ground blanched
  almonds
1 pound confectioners' sugar
1 teaspoon almond extract
4 tablespoons orange juice
1 egg white

Icing:
1 cup confectioners' sugar
1½ tablespoons orange juice
  Candied cherries, halved
  Angelica, cut in strips

Mix together almonds,
confectioners' sugar, almond
extract, and orange juice.
Knead until thoroughly blended.
Shape into a large, flat
rectangle. Wrap in aluminum
foil and chill for several hours.
Divide dough in half. Roll out
to a thickness of ⅛″ on a
board heavily dusted with
confectioners' sugar. Cut out
hearts, using 2″ heart cutter.
Cut centers out of half of the
hearts, using a smaller heart
cookie cutter. Place whole
hearts on a well buttered cookie
sheet. Top with heart-shaped
rims. Press together with
prongs of a fork. Bake in very
hot oven (450°) until lightly
browned. Brush with egg
white. Cool thoroughly. For
icing, mix confectioners' sugar
and orange juice until smooth.
Frost centers with icing.
Decorate with cherry halves
and angelica strips.

'Bee sting' cake

Bienenstich

One 15″ × 10″ × 1″ cake

>   1 package hot roll mix
>   1 cup margarine or butter
>   1 cup sugar
>   1 (6 oz.) package slivered
>   almonds

Prepare hot roll mix according
to package directions. After
first rising, knead and roll into
a large rectangle about 15″ × 10″.
Place in a buttered pan of equal
size. Put dough in a warm
place and allow the dough
to double in volume, about
20–30 minutes. Melt margarine.
Pour ¼ cup over the surface of
the dough. Add sugar to the
rest of the margarine and beat
until the sugar is dissolved.
Mix in almonds. Spread
mixture on top of buttered
dough. Bake in a moderate oven
(350°) for 35–40 minutes or
until the top is lightly browned.
Cool and cut in squares.

Fresh plum cake

Zwetschgendatschi

One 9″ × 13″ cake

>   2 pounds fresh blue plums
>   1 package dry yeast
>   1 cup milk, lukewarm
>   3½ cups flour
>   1 teaspoon salt
>   1 cup sugar
>   ¼ cup margarine or butter
>   1 egg, slightly beaten
>   2 tablespoons margarine or
>   butter

Wash and gently cut plums in
half, removing the pits. Sprinkle
yeast into ¼ cup of the milk.
Let stand until dissolved.

Mix flour, salt, and ⅓ cup of
the sugar in a large bowl. Stir
dissolved yeast, margarine, egg,
and remaining milk into flour.
Knead into a soft dough.
Let rise for 30–40 minutes in a
warm place. Punch down and
roll on a lightly floured board
into an oblong about 9″ × 13″.
Fit into a greased pan of that
size. Pinch edges to make a
slight edge around all sides.
Let rise for 20 minutes. Place
plums on top with cut side up.
Sprinkle with remaining sugar;
dot with margarine. Bake in a
moderate oven (350°) for
35–40 minutes. Slice and
serve warm.

Cherry cake

Thüringer Kirschkuchen

One 10″ cake

>   1 (16 oz.) can sour cherries,
>   pitted
>   4 eggs, separated
>   1 cup sugar
>   1 teaspoon grated lemon rind
>   1½ cups flour
>   1½ teaspoons baking powder
>   ½ teaspoon salt
>   1 teaspoon cinnamon
>   1 (6 oz.) package almonds
>   finely chopped
>   1 tablespoon margarine or
>   butter
>   ¼ cup fine dry bread crumbs

Drain cherries, reserving ½ cup
juice. Beat egg yolks, gradually
adding sugar, lemon rind, and
cherry juice. Sift flour, baking
powder, salt, and cinnamon
together. Stir flour into egg yolk
mixture, blending well. Beat
egg whites until stiff, but not
dry. Gently fold egg whites
into batter. Fold in chopped
almonds. Pour into 10″ bundt
pan, well buttered, and then
sprinkled with dry bread
crumbs. Sprinkle cherries evenly
over top. Bake in moderate
oven (350°) for 45–50 minutes,
or until cake is lightly browned
and springs back when gently
touched with finger.

Fresh plum cake

Silesian cheese cases

Schlesische Käsetaschen

6 servings

- 1 *(10 oz.) package frozen puff paste patty shells, thawed*
- 1 *(3 oz.) package cream cheese, softened*
- ½ *cup creamed cottage cheese*
- 2 *tablespoons sugar*
- ½ *cup raisins*
- 1 *egg yolk*

Roll out patty shells to approximately 8″ diameter. Beat together cream cheese, cottage cheese, sugar, raisins and egg yolk. Divide cheese filling in 6 equal portions, placing one in center of each round. Bring 6 equidistant points on outer edge to center, one at a time, moistening with water and pressing together lightly to seal. Place cases on ungreased cookie sheet. Preheat oven to 450°. Place cookie sheet into oven and immediately lower temperature to 375°. Bake until golden brown, about 30 minutes. Remove from cookie sheet. If desired, drizzle a glaze of 1 cup confectioners' sugar mixed with 1–2 tablespoons water over cases while still warm. Cool.

Fried cheese cakes

Quark-Keilchen

6 servings

- 2 *cups (1 lb.) creamed cottage cheese*
- ½ *cup dehydrated potato flakes*
- 2 *eggs*
- ⅛ *teaspoon salt*
- ⅓ *cup sugar*
- ½ *teaspoon grated lemon rind*
- ⅓ *cup raisins*
- 1 *cup sifted flour*
- ¼ *cup margarine or butter Confectioners' sugar, syrup or preserves*

Mix together cottage cheese, potato flakes, eggs, salt, sugar, lemon rind, raisins and flour to form a smooth dough, adding a little more flour if dough is too sticky. Pat the dough out on a floured surface to form a rectangle 9″ × 3″. Cut into 1½″ squares. Melt margarine in frying pan over medium heat. Fry squares on both sides until browned, about 1–2 minutes on each side. Serve hot with confectioners' sugar, syrup or preserves.

Black forest cherry cake

Schwarzwälder Kirschtorte

One 8″ layer cake

½ cup margarine or butter
½ cup sugar
3 eggs
½ cup almonds, finely chopped
   in blender
1 (6 oz.) package semi-sweet
   chocolate pieces, chopped
   fine in blender
1 teaspoon vanilla
¾ cup sifted cake flour
1 teaspoon baking powder
½ teaspoon salt
1 cup heavy cream
2 tablespoons honey
½ cup Kirschwasser or ½ cup
   cherry brandy
2 (1 lb.) cans sour pitted
   well-drained
   Maraschino cherries

Cream together margarine and
sugar until light and fluffy; add
eggs one at a time, beating well
after each addition. Beat in
almonds, ¾ cup of the chopped
chocolate, and vanilla. Sift
together flour, baking powder
and salt. Stir into butter mixture.
Divide evenly between three
greased, waxed-paper-lined and
re-greased 8″ layer cake pans.
Bake in a moderately hot oven
(375°) about 20 minutes, or until
edges start to pull away from
sides of pan. Cool on cake rack
about 10 minutes. Turn out;
remove waxed paper. Cool cake
layers on cake rack. Whip
cream with honey until stiff.
Place one cake layer on serving
plate; sprinkle with one-third
of the liquer; spread with
one-third of the whipped cream;

Black forest cherry cake

cover evenly with one-half of
the sour cherries. Place second
layer on top, pressing down
slightly. Repeat as for first
layer. Top with third layer,
press down slightly, sprinkle
with liquer, cover with whipped
cream. Decorate top and sides
with reserved ¼ cup chopped
chocolate and Maraschino
cherries. Chill well before
serving.

Chocolate layer cake

Prinzregententorte

One 8″ cake

1 (17-oz.) package pound
   cake mix
½ cup softened margarine or
   butter
1 (6-oz.) package semi-sweet
   chocolate pieces, melted
2 eggs, separated
1 cup sifted confectioners'
   sugar
3 squares unsweetened
   chocolate, melted

Prepare cake mix according to
package directions. Bake as
follows: Grease and line with
waxed paper, grease again, two
8″ round cake pans. Pour ¾ cup
(1/5 of the batter) into each
pan, spreading evenly. Bake in
moderate oven (350°) until
golden brown and edges pull
away from sides of pan, about
30 minutes. Remove from pan
and carefully peel off paper.
Cool on rack. Bake three more
layers in this way.

Filling: Beat margarine into
melted semi-sweet chocolate.
Add egg yolks; beat until
mixture is glossy and of
spreading consistency. Spread
filling between layers; press
each layer down firmly.
Cool until well set before
frosting cake.

Frosting: Beat egg whites until
foamy; beat in confectioners'
sugar gradually, until well
blended. Stir in melted
unsweetened chocolate. Spread
over top and sides of cake. Cool.

Dresden Christmas fruit bread

Dresdener Christstollen

2 loaves

2 envelopes dry yeast
1 cup lukewarm milk
5 to 5½ cups sifted flour
2 eggs
½ teaspoon salt
½ teaspoon almond extract
1 cup margarine or butter, softened
½ cup sugar
¼ cup chopped candied lemon or orange peel
⅔ cup seedless raisins
⅔ cup dried currants
½ cup slivered, blanched almonds
½ cup melted margarine or butter
⅔ cup confectioners' sugar

In mixing bowl, stir yeast into milk. Stir to dissolve. Add 4 cups of the flour, eggs, salt and almond extract; beat until smooth dough is formed. Sprinkle with about 1 tablespoon of the flour. Let stand in a warm place until doubled in bulk, about 30–45 minutes. Punch dough down, place on a lightly floured surface, knead in softened margarine, sugar, and remaining flour until smooth and well-blended. Knead in lemon or orange peel, raisins, currants and almonds. Divide into two equal portions. Roll out each to an oval shape about ¾" thick and 9" × 6" at the widest points. Fold one long side about ¾ of the way over the other. Gently press the edges together to make a loaf about 3–3½" wide by 9" long. Place on a greased baking sheet, cover and let rise in a warm place until doubled in bulk, about 30–45 minutes. Brush tops with half of the melted margarine. Bake in a moderately hot oven (400°) about 25–35 minutes or until golden brown. Brush with remaining margarine. Sprinkle with confectioners' sugar. Return to oven for 1 minute. Remove. Cool on rack.

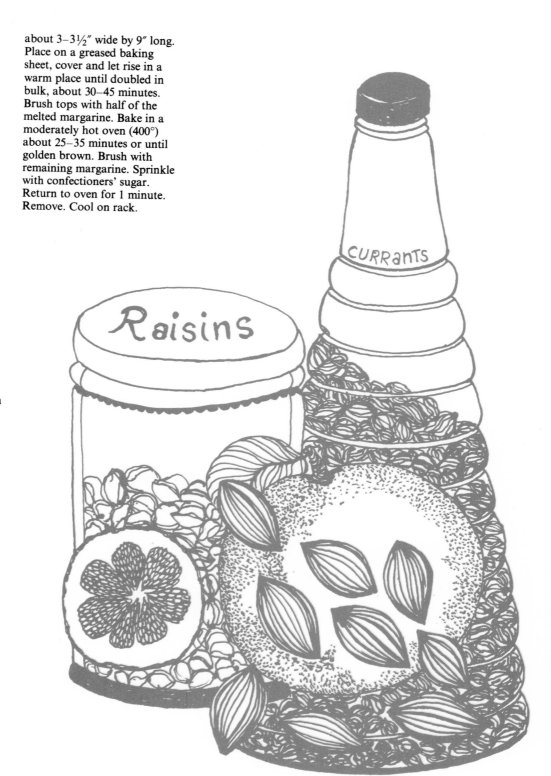

Streusel coffee cake

Streuselkuchen

One 13″ × 9″ cake

    1 package hot roll mix
    ¼ cup margarine or butter,
       melted
    1 cup flour
    1 cup sugar
    2 teaspoons cinnamon
    1 teaspoon grated lemon rind
    ½ cup margarine or butter

Prepare hot roll mix according
to package directions. After first
rising, knead and roll into
large rectangle 13″ × 9″. Fit into
a buttered pan of equal size.
Brush top with melted
margarine. Put in warm place
until dough rises to double
original size. Combine flour,
sugar, cinnamon, and lemon
rind. Cut in margarine with
pastry blender or two knives.
Spread over surface of
buttered dough. Bake in
moderate oven (350°) for 40–45
minutes or until browned.

*In old-fashioned German
families, the table is set with
beautiful lace or embroidered
tablecloths and with the best
silverware and china. The
German housewife puts her heart
and soul into these homemade
cakes and tarts. Even those who
don't happen to be very good cooks
are almost invariably good bakers.*

Delicate sour cream cake

Feiner Sahnekuchen

One 9″ × 13″ × 2″ cake

    1 (13¾ oz.) package hot roll
       mix
    2 tablespoons soft margarine
       or butter
    ½ cup sugar
    1 pint sour cream
    4 tablespoons sugar
    1 teaspoon vanilla

Prepare hot roll mix according
to package directions, adding
margarine and ½ cup sugar
when adding the egg called for
in package directions. Cover;
allow to rise in a warm place
until doubled in size, about
30–45 minutes. Knead lightly
on a floured surface several
times until dough is no longer
sticky. Roll or press out with
fingers to fit a buttered
9″ × 13″ × 2″ pan. Place in pan.
Mix together sour cream,
sugar and vanilla. Spread over
surface of dough. Let rise in
warm place until doubled,
about 30–45 minutes. Bake in a
moderate oven (350°) about
35–45 minutes or until edges
are browned. Allow to cool at
least 30 minutes before cutting
into squares.

Spicy fruit loaf

Hutzelbrot

One 9″ × 5″ × 3″ loaf

    1 (12 oz.) package pitted,
       mixed, dried fruit, diced
    ¼ cup raisins
    2 cups boiling water
    3 cups biscuit-type baking mix
    ⅔ cup sugar
    ⅓ cup flour
    1 teaspoon cinnamon
    ⅛ teaspoon ground cloves
    1 egg
    ⅔ cup milk
    ⅓ cup Kümmel, Kirschwasser
       or fruit juice
    ½ cup chopped nuts
    1 tablespoon granulated
       sugar or 1 cup confectioners'
       sugar

In a bowl, pour boiling water
over prepared fruit and raisins.
Let stand while batter is being
mixed. Stir together well,
baking mix, sugar, flour,
cinnamon and cloves. Add egg,
milk and liquer or fruit juice.
Beat vigorously about ½ minute
or until well-blended. Drain
fruit; reserve liquid. Stir fruit
and nuts into batter. Pour
batter into greased 9″ × 5″ × 3″
loaf pan. Bake in a moderate
oven (350°) about 1 hour or
until toothpick inserted near
center comes out clean. Cool
10 minutes in pan. Remove
from pan. Brush with reserved
soaking liquid; sprinkle 1
tablespoon granulated sugar
over surface while hot. Cool.
(Or, stir together 1 cup
confectioners' sugar and 1–2
tablespoons liquid drained
from fruit and 1 teaspoon liquer,
if desired. Blend well. Glaze
top of cake, letting mixture
dribble down sides. Cool.)

Berlin style jelly doughnuts

Berliner Pfannkuchen

Makes 18–20

3½ cups flour
 ¼ cup sugar
  1 teaspoon salt
  1 package yeast
  1 cup milk, lukewarm
  2 tablespoons salad oil
  1 egg, slightly beaten
  2 teaspoons rum
  1 egg white, slightly beaten
     Marmalade
     Oil or fat for deep frying
  1 cup confectioners' sugar

Sift flour, sugar and salt. Soften yeast in ¼ cup of the warm milk. Stir in ¾ of flour mixture. Add oil, egg, and rum. Add remaining flour mixture. Work into soft dough. Cover and let rise in a warm place for 45 minutes to 1 hour. Punch down and roll out on floured board into ½″ thickness. Cut into 3″ rounds. Place 1 teaspoon of marmalade in center of each round. Brush edges with egg white. Pinch edges together to seal completely. Place balls on floured surface, smooth side up; let rise 20 minutes. Heat oil to 360°; fry doughnuts a few at a time until browned on one side then turn over (about 3–4 minutes on each side). Remove from oil with slotted spoon and drain on paper towels. Sprinkle with confectioners' sugar.

You used to be able to buy Berlin doughnuts along the streets from a man pushing a small cart bearing large lined glass jars. The glass was always misted in winter because of the steam from the hot cakes inside.

Desserts

'Beggar's' apple pudding

Frankfurter Bettelmann

6 servings

- 10 slices day-old pumpernickel
  or rye bread, cubed
- 1–1½ cups apple cider
- 1 teaspoon cinnamon
- ⅓ cup sugar
- 2 pounds apples, peeled,
  cored, and sliced
- ¼ cup raisins
- 2 tablespoons margarine or
  butter

Mix bread cubes with enough
cider to moisten and soften.
Combine cinnamon and sugar.
Alternate layers of bread,
apple slices, cinnamon, sugar,
and raisins in a 2-qt. buttered
casserole. End with a top layer
of bread cubes. Dot top with
margarine. Bake in moderate
oven (350°) for 45 minutes.
Serve with cream or vanilla
ice cream.

Cranberry pudding

Pommersche Götterspeise

4 servings

- ½ cup cream
- ¾ tablespoon sugar
- ¼ teaspoon vanilla
- 2 slices pumpernickel or rye bread, crumbed
- ⅔ cup whole cranberry sauce
- 1 tablespoon pistachio nuts

Whip the cream, gently adding sugar and vanilla. Make alternate layers of bread crumbs, cranberry sauce, and whipped cream in four dessert dishes. Chill thoroughly, at least two hours. Garnish with chopped nuts.

You can make this delicious dessert with cranberries, but in Germany one always uses 'Preisselbeeren', small red berries that grow on low bushes in the woods.

'Poor Knight's' dessert

Arme Ritter

6 servings

- 1 cup milk
- 2 eggs, beaten
- 4 tablespoons sugar
- 1 teaspoon vanilla
- ½ teaspoon grated lemon rind
- 6 slices day-old white bread
- ⅓ cup dry bread crumbs
- 2 tablespoons margarine or butter
- ⅓ cup sugar
- ½ teaspoon cinnamon

Mix together milk, eggs, sugar, vanilla, and lemon rind. Dip bread slices first in egg mixture, then in dry bread crumbs. Melt margarine in large skillet and brown bread slices on both sides. Sprinkle with mixture of sugar and cinnamon. Serve warm.

Rye, pumpernickel and even white bread are often used in such hearty German desserts as 'Beggar's' apple pudding, see page 82; "Cranberry" pudding, see page 83; 'Poor Knight's dessert', and Rye bread and fruit pudding, this page.

Rye bread and fruit pudding

Bielefelder Schwarzbrotpudding

8–10 servings

- 3 eggs, separated
- ⅔ cup sugar
- 1 teaspoon vanilla
- ½ teaspoon cinnamon
- 4 cups (6 slices) seedless rye bread, cubed
- 1 pint fresh blueberries or cranberries
- 1 (6-oz.) package semi-sweet chocolate pieces
  Half-and-half, if desired

Beat egg whites until foamy. Gradually beat in ⅓ cup of the sugar and the vanilla, until stiff, but not dry. Beat egg yolks until thick; gradually beat in ⅓ cup of the sugar and cinnamon until mixture is very thick and forms a ribbon when beater is picked up. Fold egg yolk mixture into egg whites. Fold egg mixture into cubed rye bread. Sprinkle half the berries in bottom of buttered 2-quart casserole. Spread one-third of bread mixture over berries. Sprinkle half of chocolate pieces over surface. Cover with another third of bread mixture. Sprinkle remaining berries over surface, cover with last third of bread mixture. Sprinkle remaining chocolate pieces on top. Cover with lid or foil. Bake in moderately slow oven (325°) for about 1 hour, or until knife inserted one inch from edge comes out clean. Cool. Unmold onto serving plate. Serve half-and-half separately.

Dark maidens in skirts

Mohrle im Hemd

4–6 servings

    1 cup margarine or butter
 2/3 cup sugar
    3 egg yolks
    1 (6 oz.) package semi-sweet
        chocolate chips
    1 cup milk
25–30 ladyfingers
    2 tablespoons rum
 1/2 cup cream, whipped

Cream margarine and sugar.
Beat in egg yolks, continuing to
beat until thoroughly blended.
Melt chocolate bits in top of
double boiler over hot (not
boiling) water. Add milk,
stirring to combine thoroughly.
Cool. Gradually add chocolate
milk to margarine mixture; stir
until thoroughly blended.
Sprinkle ladyfingers with rum.
In a deep 2-qt. casserole, arrange
alternate layers of ladyfingers
and chocolate mixture. Chill
thoroughly. Decorate with
whipped cream. Serve cold.

Drowned maidens

Versoffene Jungfern

Makes about 4 dozen

    3 tablespoons margarine or
        butter
 1/3 cup sugar
    6 eggs, separated
 2/3 cup sifted flour
 1/2 teaspoon salt
        Oil for deep frying
        Confectioners' sugar

Cream margarine; gradually
beat in sugar until well blended.
Beat in egg yolks until smooth
and thickened. Blend in flour
and salt gently to form a smooth
batter. Beat egg whites until stiff
but not dry; fold into batter.
Drop batter by teaspoonfuls
into hot fat (400°). Fry until
golden brown, about 1–2
minutes on each side, turning
once. Drain on paper towels;
sprinkle with confectioners'
sugar. Serve immediately.

Brandied plum mold

Cognac Pflaumenpudding

4–6 servings

1 (30 oz.) can purple plums
2 envelopes unflavored gelatine
½ cup cold water
¼ cup sugar
1 teaspoon grated lemon rind
¼ cup lemon juice
⅓ cup plum or cherry brandy
¼ teaspoon cinnamon
1 teaspoon vanilla
½ cup chopped almonds
½ cup heavy cream, whipped

Drain plums; reserve and measure liquid. Pit and purée the plums in blender or through a food mill. Soften gelatine in cold water. Heat 1¾ cups plum liquid and sugar to the boiling point, stirring frequently; remove from heat. Stir in softened gelatine until dissolved. Stir in 1⅔ cups plum purée, lemon rind and juice, brandy, cinnamon and vanilla. Pour into 1½ quart mold which has been rinsed with cold water. Chill until firmly set, about 2–3 hours. Unmold on serving platter. Garnish with almonds and whipped cream.

Brandied plum mold

Munich beer cream

Munich beer cream

Münchner Biercreme

6 servings

1 cup mild dark beer
¾ cup water
½ cup sugar
2 tablespoons lemon juice
1 tablespoon unflavored gelatine
4 eggs, separated

In top of a double boiler, mix together beer, ½ cup of the water, sugar, and lemon juice. Sprinkle gelatine over remaining ¼ cup of water; mix to dissolve; add to beer mixture. Beat egg yolks slightly and stir into beer mixture. Place over simmering water. Cook, stirring constantly, until mixture coats a metal spoon, about 8–10 minutes. Cool. Beat egg whites until they stand in soft peaks. Fold egg whites into beer mixture. Pour into individual serving dishes and chill. Serve cold.

White grape custard

Saarländer Becher

6–8 servings

- ½ cup seedless white grapes, halved
- ½ cup sugar
- 1 tablespoon cornstarch
- 1 teaspoon grated lemon rind
- 1 tablespoon lemon juice
- 2 cups sauterne wine
- 4 eggs, lightly beaten
  Crisp rolled cookies

Divide grapes among individual serving dishes or place in serving bowl. Mix sugar and cornstarch in top section of double boiler. Stir in lemon rind, lemon juice and wine. Cook over direct medium heat, stirring constantly, until mixture comes to a boil. Pour about half of the cooked mixture over the beaten eggs, stirring rapidly to blend. Return egg mixture to top of double boiler, blending with remaining wine mixture. Cook over hot but *not* boiling water, stirring constantly, until mixture thickens and coats a spoon, about 1 minute. Strain immediately and pour over grapes. Serve warm or chilled with a crisp rolled cookie.

White grape custard

Currant and raspberry pudding

Rote Grütze

4 servings

- 1 (10-oz.) package quick-thaw frozen raspberries, thawed
- 1 (4-oz.) package currant and raspberry flavor pudding mix
  Light cream or half-and-half

Drain juice from frozen raspberries, measure and add water to make 2 cups. **DO NOT USE MILK.** Stir into pudding mix in saucepan. Bring to a boil. Boil one minute only, stirring constantly. Very gently, stir in drained raspberries. Pour into individual serving dishes. Chill 3 to 4 hours. Serve with cream or half-and-half.

Beverages

The average German is evidently a thirsty man. Not only does he drink 140 liters of beer and 18 liters of wine per year, but Germany is also famous for its cold and warm fruit punch. During the summer, signs hanging in the gardens of the cafes along the Rhine, Moselle and Neckar rivers announce: 'cherry punch today'. On the white Rhine boats, the waiter prowls the deck with large glass mugs, set in bowls with crushed ice and filled with sparkling, full-flavored 'Kalte Ente', a delicious drink made of white wine and fruit. Hot drinks such as 'Krambambuli' and 'Feuerzwangenbowl' were always the reward of hunters after they reached the comfort of their firesides on winter nights in their remote castles in the woods of East Prussia or Schleswig-Holstein.
These drinks were considered too strong for the ladies, however.
These same hot and potent drinks were traditional for warming up the student parties in Heidelberg when it was still the exclusive university for the sons of aristocrats. But that time is long gone. Krambambuli, Jägerspunch and Feuerzwangenbowl are still prepared and drunk, but the company is less exclusive and the ladies enjoy them now as well.

Krambambuli

Krambambuli

18 servings

  ½ gallon dry red wine
  ¼ cup orange juice
  2 tablespoons lemon juice
  1 spiral orange peel
  1 stick cinnamon
  4 cloves
  8 tablespoons sugar
  ⅓ cup rum

Combine wine, juice, peel, cinnamon, cloves and 4 tablespoons sugar in saucepan. Simmer 8–10 minutes; strain into punch bowl. Heat rum slightly. Place remaining sugar in large metal spoon or ladle. Light rum with a match; pour over sugar. Pour burning sugar over punch.

Peach cup

Pfirsich-bowle

16 servings

  4 ripe peaches, peeled, pitted and quartered
  ¼ to ½ cup super fine sugar
  ½ cup brandy
  2 bottles Rhine wine
  1 quart chilled club soda

Place fruit in large pitcher; sprinkle with sugar. Add brandy; stir well. Stir in wine. Cover; chill 2–3 hours. Add club soda just before serving.

Cold duck

Kalte Ente

18 servings

  ½ cup super fine sugar
  1 large lemon, thinly sliced and seeded
  ½ cup orange liqueur
  ½ gallon Rhine wine, chilled
    Ice
  1 (12 oz.) bottle club soda, chilled

Sprinkle sugar over lemon slices. Press lemon slices with back of spoon to release flavor. Stir in orange liqueur. Chill. Stir in wine; pour over ice in punch bowl. Add club soda; stir lightly to blend.

Hunters' punch

Jägerpunch

12 servings

    1 bottle Rhine wine
    2 cups water
    1 spiral lemon peel
    2 cloves
    1 stick cinnamon
    2 tablespoons sugar
    2 teaspoons instant tea
  ¼ cup rum

Combine wine, water, lemon peel, cloves, cinnamon and sugar in saucepan. Simmer 10–12 minutes. Stir in tea and rum. Strain before serving. Serve hot.

Hot seal

Heißer Seehund

8 servings

    1 bottle Rhine wine
 1¾ cup seedless golden raisins
    1 stick cinnamon
    1 spiral lemon peel
  ¼ cup sugar
  ¼ cup brandy

Combine wine, raisins, cinnamon, lemon peel, and sugar in saucepan. Simmer 8–10 minutes. Remove lemon peel. Add brandy. Ladle into individual punch cups.

Bowles

A warm afternoon or evening calls for a very cool, very refreshing but not too heady drink. One that's low on alcohol, takes little work, provides a relaxing atmosphere and tastes delightful. That means a punch.

Germans have realized the entertainment impact of punches or Bowles, as they're called, for centuries. And rightly so, since the light, white wines from vineyards dating back to the Romans are ideally suited for such beverages. Low in alcohol, they have a fruity character all their own which compliments the fruit used in the recipe.

The Bowle (pronounced Beau-la) can be prepared beforehand and created in dozens of variations that not only taste delicious but look appetizing.

There's an art, of course, to making the perfect Bowle.

First: The Wine –

To be authentic, with the perfect balance between fruit and wine it must be a German white wine. Germany has 11 regions producing wines, and two of the three types mentioned in the recipes used here – Rhine wine and Moselle wine – are generic names of wines of two of these regions.

They're easy to find anywhere German wines are sold. A long-necked brown bottle, for example, indicates a full-bodied Rhine wine; a green bottle, with a similar long neck, contains a light and delicate wine from the Moselle-Saar-Ruwer region.

(There's another green bottle used but this one, called "Bocksbeutel" by Germans, is short, flagon-shaped and holds dry and robust wines from still another region – Franconia.)

The third wine type – Sekt – is a sparkling wine, which comes in the traditional over-size bottle used for this type of beverage.

Second: The Technique –

1. Chill wines first.

2. Use sugar sparingly . . . you don't want to overpower the delicate flavor of the wine. If sweetened fruits are to be added, use less sugar at the beginning. Dissolve sugar completely in a small amount of wine; then stir in with the rest of the ingredients.

3. Never add cloudy fruit juices or mashed fruit. A Bowle is a clear beverage; the fruits should be firm, but ripe.

4. Mix Bowle ingredients just before serving. Or if mixing in advance, keep covered so the lovely aroma will not escape.

5. Do NOT dilute with ice cubes. Place the punch bowl in a larger bowl of ice-and-water. Or keep pitchers in ice-and-water-filled tubs.

6. To serve, it's best to use a glass, plastic or ceramic ladle. If metal ladles are used, do not let them stand in the punch bowl.

Orange Punch

Apflesinen bowle

24 servings

  3 oranges
  ¼ cup sugar
  3 bottles chilled Rhine or Moselle wine
  2 cups club soda

Grate rind from one of the oranges; place rind in a bowl. Peel that orange and the other two oranges. Section peeled oranges and add to bowl with sugar and 1 bottle of the wine. Chill. Just before serving, stir in remaining two bottles of wine and the club soda. Oranges will begin to float to the top shortly after club soda is added.

Pineapple Punch

Ananas bowle

22 servings

  2 cups diced fresh ripe pineapple
  ¼ cup sugar
  2 bottles chilled Rhine wine
  1 bottle chilled Sekt

Combine pineapple, sugar, and 1 bottle of the Rhine wine. Cover and let stand at room temperature several hours. Then chill. To serve, stir in remaining bottle of Rhine wine and the Sekt. Pineapple pieces will float to top as soon as Sekt is added.

Strawberry Punch

Erdbeer bowle

32 servings
  1 pint strawberries
  ¼ cup sugar
  4 bottles chilled Moselle wine
  ½ bottle chilled Sekt or 2 cups club soda (optional)

Cut strawberries in half. Sprinkle with sugar and refrigerate for several hours. Place strawberries and any juice that has formed in the bottom of a punch bowl or in several pitchers. Add wine and Sekt. Serve immediately.

NOTE: Sekt is German sparkling wine, reflecting all the characteristics of Rhine and Moselle wines, with the added benefit of effervescence.

Raspberry Punch

Himbeer bowle

Use the recipe for Erdbeer Bowle, substituting whole raspberries for the halved strawberries.

Kitchen terms

Aspic
A stiff gelatine obtained by combining fish or meat bouillon with gelatine powder.

Au gratin
Obtained by covering a dish with a white sauce (usually prepared with grated cheese) and then heating the dish in the oven so that a golden crust forms.

Baste
To moisten meat or other foods while cooking to add flavor and to prevent drying of the surface. The liquid is usually melted fat, meat drippings, fruit juice or sauce.

Blanch (precook)
To preheat in boiling water or steam. (1) Used to inactivate enzymes and shrink food for canning, freezing, and drying. Vegetables are blanched in boiling water or steam, and fruits in boiling fruit juice, sirup, water, or steam. (2) Used to aid in removal of skins from nuts, fruits, and some vegetables.

Blend
To mix thoroughly two or more ingredients.

Bouillon
Brown stock, conveniently made by dissolving a bouillon cube in water.

Broth
Water in which meat, fish or vegetables have been boiled or cooked.

'En papillote'
Meat, fish or vegetables wrapped in grease-proof paper or aluminum foil (usually first sprinkled with oil or butter, herbs and seasonings) and then baked in the oven or grilled over charcoal. Most of the taste and aroma are preserved in this way.

Fold
To combine by using two motions, cutting vertically through the mixture and turning over and over by sliding the implement across the bottom of the mixing bowl with each turn.

Fry
To cook in fat; applied especially (1) to cooking in a small amount of fat, also called sauté or pan-fry; (2) to cooking in a deep layer of fat, also called deep-fat frying.

Marinate
To let food stand in a marinade usually an oil–acid mixture like French dressing.

Parboil
To boil until partially cooked. The cooking is usually completed by another method.

Poach
To cook in a hot liquid using precautions to retain shape. The temperature used varies with the food.

Reduce
To concentrate the taste and aroma of a particular liquid or food e.g. wine, bouillon, soup, sauce etc. by boiling in a pan with the lid off so that the excess water can evaporate.

Roast
To cook, uncovered, by dry heat. Usually done in an oven, but occasionally in ashes, under coals or on heated stones or metals. The term is usually applied to meats but may refer to other food as potatoes, corn, chestnuts.

Sauté
To brown or cook in a small amount of fat. See Fry.

Simmer
To cook in a liquid just below the boiling point, at temperatures of 185°–210°. Bubbles form slowly and collapse below the surface.

Skim
To take away a layer of fat from soup, sauces, etc.

Stock
The liquid in which meat or fish has been boiled together with herbs and vegetables.

Whip
To beat rapidly to produce expansion, due to incorporation of air as applied to cream, eggs, and gelatin dishes.

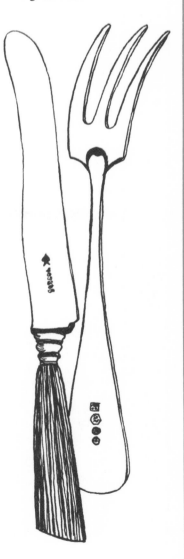

Conversion tables

American			metric equivalent
standard cup			(approximately)
1 cup = $\frac{1}{2}$ pint	= 8 fl. oz. (fluid ounce)	= 2,37 dl (deciliter)
1 tbs. (tablespoon)	= $\frac{1}{2}$ fl. oz.	= 1,5 cl (centiliter)
1 tsp. (teaspoon)	= $\frac{1}{6}$ fl. oz.	= 0,5 cl
1 pint	= 16 fl. oz.	= 4,73 dl
1 quart = 2 pints	= 32 fl. oz.	= 9,46 dl

British		metric equivalent
standard cup		(approximately)
1 cup = $\frac{1}{2}$ pint	= 10 fl. oz.	= 2,84 dl
1 tbs	= 0.55 fl. oz.	= 1,7 cl
1 tsp.	= $\frac{1}{5}$ fl. oz.	= 0,6 cl
1 pint	= 20 fl. oz.	= 5,7 dl
1 quart = 2 pints	= 40 fl. oz.	= 1,1 l (liter)

1 cup = 16 tablespoons
1 tablespoon = 3 teaspoons

1 liter = 10 deciliter = 100 centiliter

Centigrade	Fahrenheit	
up to 105° C	up to 225° F	cool
105–135° C	225–275° F	very slow
135–160° C	275–325° F	slow
175–190° C	350–375° F	moderate
215–230° C	400–450° F	hot
230–260° C	450–500° F	very hot
260° C	500° F	extremely hot

Solid measures

American/British		metric equivalent
		(approximately)
1 lb. (pound)	= 16 oz. (ounces)	= 453 g (gram)
	1 oz.	= 28 g
2.2 lbs.		= 1000 g = 1 kg (kilogram)
	$3\frac{1}{2}$ oz.	= 100 g

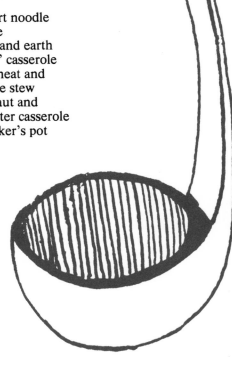